history skills

FOR NCEA LEVEL 1

The past is another country: skills for helping you navigate it

GRAEME BALL

Australia • Brazil • Japan • Korea • Mexico • Singapore • Spain • United Kingdom • United States

History Skills NCEA Level 1 Workbook
1st Edition
Graeme Ball

Cover designer: Cheryl Smith, Macarn Design
Text designer: Cheryl Smith, Macarn Design
Production controller: Siew Han Ong
Reprint: Jennifer Foo

Any URLs contained in this publication were checked for currency during the production process. Note, however, that the publisher cannot vouch for the ongoing currency of URLs.

Acknowledgements
Cover image: Wrecked car on Washington, D.C. street in 1922. Everett Historical Collection.
Public domain images Page 4, poster for the film The Time Machine (1960 film). Page 28 Suffrage poster: 'Read our paper. Votes for women', 1920. Page 44, Photographer Jessie Tarbox Beals standing next to her camera (on tripod), with camera trigger in hand, 1905. Page 45, Photographing Goldi shaman on the Amur River, north of Khabarovsk, 1895. Page 46, Fanning family, 1895. Native American Indians of the Columbia Plateau on horses in front of tipis, 1908. Page 48, United States Information Agency photograph of the March on Washington, August 28, 1963; Page 50, A French assault on German positions. Champagne, France, 1917. Page 51, Woman suffrage headquarters in Upper Euclid Avenue, Cleveland, 1912. Page 54, Ballarat Street, Queenstown, NZ, flooded 1878, William P. Hart (1845 - 1926). Page 55, Lancashire Fusiliers of the 125th Brigade, 42nd (East Lancashire) Division, bound for Cape Helles, Gallipoli, May 1915. Page 57, altered photographs of Josef Stalin, Ulysses S. Grant, Benito Mussolini (unidentified photographers, public domain). Page 64, US Library of Congress, attributed to Hine Lewis Wickes (1874-1940). Page 65, At Last a Perfect Soldier! by Robert Minor. First published on the back cover of The Masses, July 1916. Page 77, Photographer unidentified, 1905. Page, 79, National Archives and Records Service, 1941. Page 90, Team photograph of the New Zealand rugby union team before playing South Africa in 1921. The South Africa rugby union side for their first ever Test match against New Zealand, at Carisbrook, Dunedin, 1921.
Shutterstock images pages 4, 5, 7, 9, 17, 21, 26, 32; 45; 61, 62, 63, 72, 89, 92, 93, 102.
Alexander Turnbull Library Page 53, Anti-Springbok Tour demonstration, Willis St, Wellington. Page 67 and 68, Peter Bromhead.
Other sources Page 6 NAC poster Don Thomas Collection. San Diego Air and Space Museum; Haere Mi poster Wellington [New Zealand]: By authority W. A. G. Skinner, Government Printer, Boston Public Library, Vintage Travel Posters; Front page of the Auckland Star Monday, July 21, 1969.; Page 27 Adam Zyglis, Buffalo News. All rights reserved. Page 47, A Boer War nurse boarding a horse-drawn RAMC supply wagon. 'Sister Pretty departing', Wellcome Trust, 1900. Page 66, 'Mobile Relationship' by Manu Cornet. Page 69, Illingworth, Leslie Gilbert, Published: Daily Mail, 29 October 1962. Page 70, Joel Pett Editorial Cartoon (used with the permission of Joel Pett and the Cartoonist Group). All rights reserved. Page 71, Khalil Bendib, OtherWords.

For product information and technology assistance,
in Australia call **1300 790 853**;
in New Zealand call **0800 449 725**

For permission to use material from this text or product, please email **aust.permissions@cengage.com**

National Library of New Zealand Cataloguing-in-Publication Data
A catalogue record for this book is available from the National Library of New Zealand

978 0 17 0352 581

Cengage Learning Australia
Level 7, 80 Dorcas Street
South Melbourne, Victoria, Australia 3205

Cengage Learning New Zealand
Unit 4B Rosedale Office Park
331 Rosedale Road, Albany, North Shore 0632, NZ

For learning solutions, visit **cengage.co.nz**

Printed in Malaysia by Papercraft
8 9 10 11 12 25 24

Contents

Inquiry skills and sources

Essay-writing skills

1 Primary and secondary sources/evidence

Types of evidence: primary and secondary

Primary

Primary evidence is anything that was created at the time of the events/period being studied. (It can also be something created *much later* by someone who was there; an example of this would be an autobiography.) Primary evidence is extremely useful to historians because it is like a time machine that takes us back to the lives of people in the past.

One way to think about primary evidence is this: if there were somehow no primary evidence, *there would be no history!* Historians were often not alive themselves at the time of the history they write about or, if they were, they did not necessarily experience it all themselves. This means that they rely on the evidence left behind by those who were there at the time. This is rather like a detective turning up at a crime scene after the crime has been committed; he or she must use the evidence that the criminal (and victim) has left behind to figure out the details of the crime.

The Auckland Star
MOON SPECIAL
HOME EXTRA
MAN'S WALK ON THE MOON
MOONSHIP DODGES ROCKY CRATER TO MAKE PERFECT LANDING
Dig may solve mystery

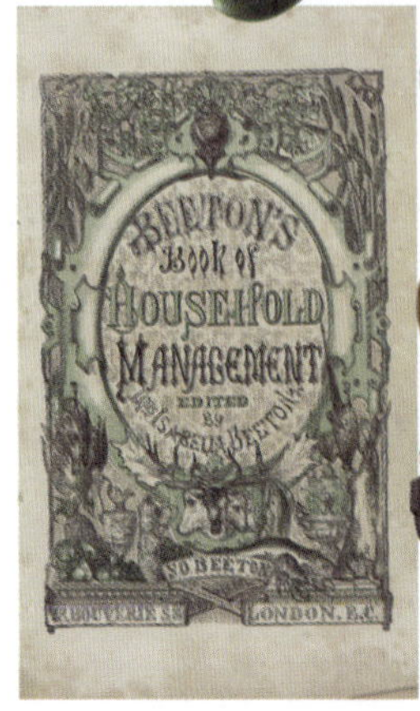

ISBN: 9780170352581

Secondary

Primary evidence is obviously vital in terms of helping us understand the past, but it often needs specialised skills to interpret it properly. Firstly, it really needs someone who already knows quite a lot about the topic to bring their understanding to it, especially if there is new primary evidence. Secondly, the person trying to make sense of the primary evidence must know how to examine it for both usefulness and reliability. Again, this is much like the detective who brings his or her skills to examine the evidence at a crime scene.

Once the historian has analysed all of the available primary evidence on their area of research, they begin to write it up. You can think of the primary evidence they've found and analysed as the pieces of a jigsaw puzzle. The historian puts together those pieces for us so that they make sense, creating a 'picture of the past' (usually in words) based on their understanding of the evidence. Mostly, this is how the rest of us come to 'know the past'. The histories produced, usually published in books, journals or turned into documentaries, are called secondary sources.

Without primary sources there would be no secondary sources, and without secondary sources most of us would find it very difficult to know much about the past beyond our own family or community.

1 ACTIVITY

Imagine that each piece of the jigsaw puzzle here represents a primary source that an historian has found.

1 From this (incomplete) collection of evidence, what do you think is this 'picture of the past'?

After collecting more primary evidence and using skills to analyse it and put it together, this historian now has a fuller understanding of the past that they are researching.

2 From this (still incomplete) collection of evidence, what do you now think is this 'picture of the past'?

____

____

____

____

This example shows how historians are careful to always gather as much primary evidence as possible before they fully write up their histories and publish them as accurate 'pictures of the past'. Therefore, confirmation of that 'picture' by many different primary sources/evidence is important. *See Chapter 5 for more on this.*

2 ACTIVITY

Identify whether the following pieces of evidence are most likely 'Primary' or 'Secondary'.

1 A letter written by a Maori chief to the Governor of New South Wales. ____________

2 A statue from the time of the (Chinese) Ming dynasty. ____________

3 A newspaper story about the 1981 Springbok tour. ____________

4 A gravestone in a cemetery. ____________

5 A car maintenance manual from 1950. ____________

6 A Nazi propaganda film. ____________

7 A handwritten recipe book kept by your grandmother. ____________

8 A scrapbook made by you while at primary school. ____________

ISBN: 9780170352581

9 A World War Two street sign advising the location of air-raid shelters. ____________

10 Court records about the trial of someone for the theft of a car. ____________

11 A poster advertising a production of Shakespeare's *Romeo and Juliet*. ____________

12 A vinyl record of early Elvis Presley songs. ____________

13 A New Zealand two-cent coin. ____________

14 A house built in 1890. ____________

15 A documentary about New Zealand nurses during World War Two. ____________

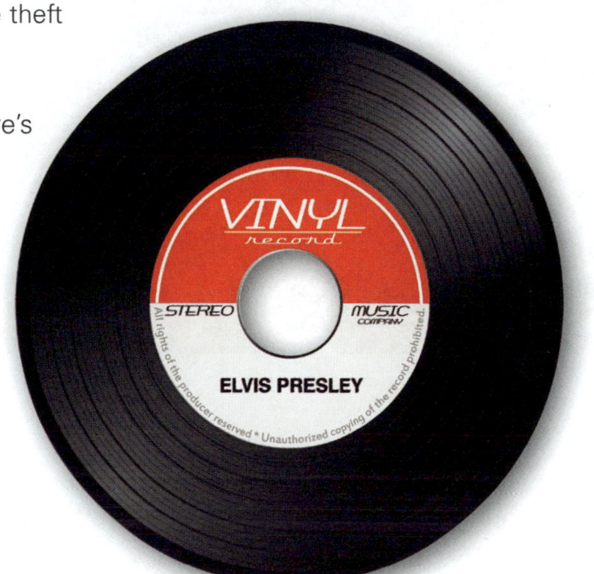

Believe it or not ...

You are currently reading a primary document, as well as creating one yourself by completing the activities in this workbook! A historian studying education in the future might well find this a very interesting source of information about what sort of things students were learning in the early part of the 21st century, and how well they were learning it.

TODAY IN HISTORY

JANUARY

1/1/1850	Pencarrow lighthouse, first in New Zealand, lights up
5/1/1977	Maori protesters begin 16-month occupation at Bastion Point
6/1/1945	Battle of the Bulge ends when Allied forces finally triumph over German firepower
9/1/1879	Parliament's term set at three years, replacing five-year term in force since 1852
9/1/1915	Allied troops begin withdrawing from Gallipoli
10/1/1863	London's Metropolitan, the world's first underground passenger rail system, opens
14/1/1878	First private telephone call is made by Queen Victoria to Thomas Biddulph
17/1/1945	Soviet troops and Polish forces liberate Warsaw (Poland) after more than five years under Nazi rule
17/1/1997	First divorce granted in Ireland
19/1/1845	Governor Fitzroy offers £100 reward for Hone Heke's capture; Heke immediately offers a similar reward for Fitzroy!
20/1/1910	Canberra becomes official capital of Australia
22/1/1875	The Taranaki settlement of Inglewood established (with a bottle of champagne smashed against a tree)
25/1/1915	Telephone inventor Alexander Graham Bell starts US transcontinental telephone service
27/1/1973	Accords are signed in Paris ending the Vietnam War
30/1/1933	Hitler appointed Chancellor

2 Recording source details

In any inquiry you do, you are required to give the details of the sources that you use, just as historians always do. This is so that anyone (including your teacher) can see where you got your information from, be it primary or secondary. It can also help another historian if they are researching a topic similar to yours and the sources you use might be useful for their work.

There is a convention *[common standard]* for recording source details of books and websites, so it's worthwhile learning it, especially if you plan to continue studying history at a higher level. Also, while a bibliography (separate list of sources used) is not required for an inquiry, we will still use the same conventions to give source details.

Recording source details for a book

The following shows the details that should be given and the way that they should be set out:

- Author's surname, author's initial(s). <u>Book title</u> (<u>underlined if handwritten</u>, *italics if typed*), publisher, city of publication, date of publication, page number(s).

Example

Smithers, J. *The Pioneering Period and Colonial Conflicts*, Victoria University Press, Wellington, 1922, pages 97–99.

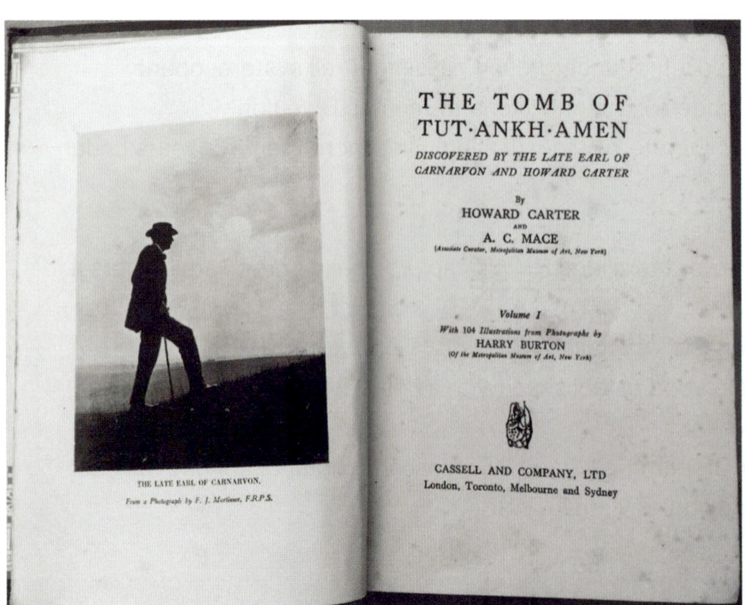

THE LATE EARL OF CARNARVON.
From a Photograph by F. J. Mortimer, F.R.P.S.

THE TOMB OF TUT·ANKH·AMEN

DISCOVERED BY THE LATE EARL OF CARNARVON AND HOWARD CARTER

By
HOWARD CARTER
AND
A. C. MACE
(Associate Curator, Metropolitan Museum of Art, New York)

Volume I
With 104 Illustrations from Photographs by
HARRY BURTON
(Of the Metropolitan Museum of Art, New York)

CASSELL AND COMPANY, LTD
London, Toronto, Melbourne and Sydney

The title page inside the front cover of the book has author details and the book's full title.

ISBN: 9780170352581

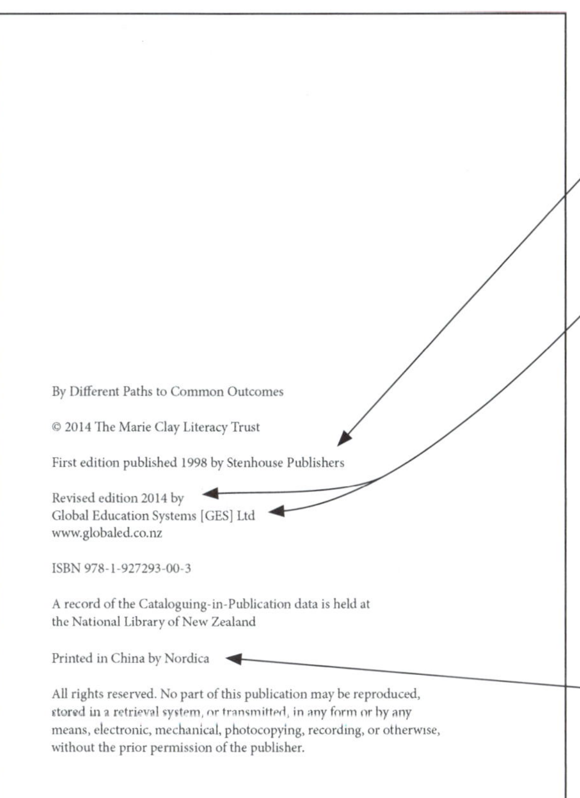

By Different Paths to Common Outcomes

© 2014 The Marie Clay Literacy Trust

First edition published 1998 by Stenhouse Publishers

Revised edition 2014 by
Global Education Systems [GES] Ltd
www.globaled.co.nz

ISBN 978-1-927293-00-3

A record of the Cataloguing-in-Publication data is held at the National Library of New Zealand

Printed in China by Nordica

All rights reserved. No part of this publication may be reproduced, stored in a retrieval system, or transmitted, in any form or by any means, electronic, mechanical, photocopying, recording, or otherwise, without the prior permission of the publisher.

Imprint page

This is the publisher of the first edition (Stenhouse Publishers) and the date of publication (1998).

This is the publisher of the *revised* edition (Global Education Systems Ltd) and the date of publication (2014). A new or revised edition of a book is an updated version, so if there are any editions noted then include in your details the **most recent date**.

We are interested in both the publisher and date published. Knowing who the publishing company is can often tell us (with some research) about the quality of the book. The publishing date effectively tells us how old the information in the book is.

This is where the book is printed; sometimes it will have one or more dates. We're not really interested in when or where the book was printed, so just ignore this information.

Recording source details for a website

Provide the URL (web address), a brief description (if possible) and the date visited.

Example

www.dnzb.govt.nz, Dictionary of New Zealand Biography, date visited: 20 March 2025

NOTE: Website source details require the date visited because websites are easily changed. If necessary, someone could retrieve from the website archive the version of the site that you visited and referenced in your inquiry *if you have provided the date visited.*

Recording source details for a documentary

Provide the title, producer (person) and production company. If you need to reference a specific part of the documentary, you can include how far in it is (in minutes).

See your teacher for advice on other types of sources.

1 ACTIVITY

Make the corrections needed for the following book source details.

- *Some details may be completely missing. If this is the case, note down what these are.*
- *Some details given below are unnecessary; cross them out.*

1 M. McKinnon, 1986, Auckland, *Independence in Foreign Policy*, Auckland University Press

2 Simpson, T. *The Sugarbag Years*, Auckland, first published 1976, reprint 1981, pp. 12–13

3 *Book of Events*, Keith Hamish, Wellington, printed in Hong Kong, Penguin, p. 45

4 Walker, R. *Struggle Without End*, Christchurch, Penguin, 1989

5 G. Scrimgeour, *The Scrim-Lee Papers*, 65 Beresford St, Auckland, Heinemann, first edition 1995, this edition 1999

6 Spencer William, Christchurch, 1990, p. 39

7 Corbett, L. *Multi-Purpose Premium*, Otago University Press, Dunedin, 1992, p. 12

8 Jason, M. *New Zealand Wars*, p. 23, Hamilton, 1992, Pearson

FINISHED?

1 'Make up' the source details of TWO books and write them out correctly.

Book source A:

Book source B:

 ISBN: 9780170352581

2 Now 'make up' the source details of TWO books and write them out INCORRECTLY. When finished, swap them with someone else to correct.

Book source 1: ______________________

Book source 2: ______________________

Correction 1: ______________________

Correction 2: ______________________

3 In a library session, select any TWO *non-fiction* books and write out the details correctly. Bring the books and your work to your teacher for checking.

Library book source 1:

Library book source 2:

TODAY IN HISTORY

FEBRUARY

3/2/1931	Hawke's Bay earthquake strikes at 10.47 am; 7.8 on the Richter scale, killing 256 people
6/2/1840	Treaty of Waitangi first signed
11/2/1882	The *Dunedin* leaves Port Chalmers with the first cargo of frozen meat, bound for Britain
660 BC	Accession to the Japanese throne of the first Emperor Jimmu – now considered Japan's founding day.
12/2/1912	Pu Yi, the 'Last Emperor', abdicates ending 2000 years of Imperial rule in China
14/2/1779	Captain Cook killed at Kealakekua Bay in Hawaii
17/2/1835	William Colenso prints the first book (a religious text) in New Zealand (in Maori)
22/2/2011	Christchurch earthquake, 6.3 magnitude, kills 185
26/2/1844	Two Wellington lawyers fight a duel with pistols. One is shot in the groin and dies a few days later
26/2/1848	*Communist Manifesto* published by Marx and Engels

ISBN: 9780170352581

3 Searching for sources of relevant information

Searching in books

Look up the **key words** from your inquiry's focusing question in your school or local library catalogue to find suitable books, magazines, journals and so on. *See page 16 for more on identifying key words.*

Contents page

Look in the Contents page (front of the book). This contains the main chapter headings, so gives you a 'big picture' view of what is in the book.

- For example, if you were looking for information on Maori leadership in New Zealand before World War Two, Chapter 3 here would probably be useful.

Contents

Index

Look in the Index (back of the book) for key words from your topic. This will allow you to go to a specific page where that information will be. The more pages on which your key words appear, the more information there will likely be on your topic.

- Here, for example, you can see that there are quite a few references in the text *Big World, Small Country* to President Roosevelt, but not a lot on the Rastafarian movement.

 ISBN: 9780170352581

Headings

Once you have found one or more pages in a book where it looks likely that there will be relevant information, quickly scan any headings that there might be. They will give you a stronger indication of what the information on the page is likely to be.

- Here, for example, if you were researching how Aborigines have been treated in Australia, the headings all signal that you've probably come to the right place. The bigger heading (at the bottom) suggests that the text is moving on to look at Aboriginal protest.

Australian government policy
As with Maori in New Zealand at the beginning of the 20th century, the Aborigines in Australia were marginalised *[side-lined]* outside mainstream …

The Stolen Generations
One of the main concerns of the Australian government was the growing number of 'mixed race' children. In 1913 a report on Aborigines recommended …

It's hard to say sorry
A 1995 report into the 'Stolen Generations' called on the government to apologise for the policy, and to provide compensation for those affected. All …

The beginnings of the protest movement

Public Aboriginal protest first occurred in 1938. While the rest of Australia was celebrating 150 years of European colonisation, a group of over 100 Aborigines carried out a Day of Mourning protest – a brave action in a time of little tolerance. In a letter sent to the Prime Minister, protestors set out their demands. These included an end to unfair treatment, return of stolen lands, equal rights (including voting), representation in the Australian parliament, recognition of Aboriginal law, and an end to the forced removal of mixed race children. Although this had …

Topic sentences

In a big page of text where there are no headings, try quickly scanning the topic sentences (they begin each paragraph). These should signal what main idea is coming up in the rest of the paragraph. You can then decide to read the rest of the paragraph or move on to the next topic sentence. This can save you an enormous amount of time.

- For example, in the rest of the first paragraph below we would expect there to be information about the reasons why Te Puea did not want Waikato Maori to fight in World War One. If this was what you were after in your research, you'd then read on. If not, you would skip to the next paragraph's topic sentence.

When World War One broke out in 1914, Te Puea argued that Waikato Maori should not fight. She felt this way for two reasons. Her grandfather, Tawhiao, had been the Maori king during the Waikato wars of the 1860s. When they came to an end, he declared that Waikato should never again fight. Te Puea intended to follow that instruction. She also saw no reason why her people should fight and die for a British king and for a New Zealand government that had taken their lands. During World War One, Te Puea was called 'the German woman' by some. This was because she was the granddaughter of William Searancke, who was (wrongly) thought to be a German. Her views and actions, and a widespread belief that she was a German sympathiser, angered many Pakeha.

When the Young Maori Party, other tribes and the government began to pressure Waikato Maori to sign up to fight, Te Puea led the resistance. This included opposition to conscription when it was introduced for Maori in 1917. Waikato and Maniapoto Maori in particular were targeted by the government. In 1918, Te Puea gathered together at Mangatawhiri those who had been balloted (called up to fight) and led the passive resistance when they were arrested. She travelled to Auckland in an attempt to visit the men imprisoned at the Narrow Neck military camp. Mokona, one of those in the camp, described how Te Puea would sit outside the prison. Often, as the men walked to the whare mimi (toilet), they were able to see her. Suddenly, everyone *'invented an excuse to go to the whare mimi. The fact that she was there gave us heart to continue.'* Because of her stand, Te Puea became a well-known figure in New Zealand.

ISBN: 9780170352581

1 ACTIVITY

Use the information on searching books to fill in the gaps.

The Contents page of a book contains ____________ ____________ headings. This is the best place to look for a '____________ ____________' overview. At the back of a book you'll find the ____________. Look here for ____________ ____________ from your topic. The more ____________ on which your key words appear, the more information there will likely be on your ____________. Once you start searching for information on the actual pages, quickly scan any ____________. They will give you a stronger ____________ of what the ____________ on the page is likely to be. In a big page of text where there are no headings, you can quickly ____________ the ____________ sentences to find out what is the ____________ idea being covered in the whole paragraph. You can then decide to ____________ the rest of the ____________ or move on to the next topic sentence!

2 ACTIVITY

1 Read the highlighted topic sentence in each of the four paragraphs below and then state *in your own words* what main idea you would expect to find further developed in the rest of the paragraph.

2 Read the rest of each paragraph. Even if you don't really understand it, is the information in it what you expected to see, based on the topic sentence?

A A revolution is a widespread, fundamental *[deep]* change in the political system, social structure, and economic control in a country. The three key revolutions of the 20th century took place in Mexico (1911–20), Russia (1917–21), and China (1935–49). At the time of their revolutions, all three countries were mainly farming economies with very little industry. Mexico's revolution was the least radical, but did produce genuine social change and political stability. Russia's saw a genuinely revolutionary movement gain power. China's revolution unified a divided country, and it was also the first in an Asian state. All three followed similar phases: disintegration of the existing political system; conflict between rival groups seeking power, leading to civil war and the victory of one of these groups; a strengthening of the power of the new government; arguments within this new government over the direction of the revolution; and, finally, the formation of a lasting political structure.

 ISBN: 9780170352581

B The Russian Revolution was perhaps the most important turning point of the 20th century. To start with, it was the first attempt in the 20th century to forcibly change human nature, to bend a whole population to the will of the political leadership. Other dictatorships elsewhere in the world — for example, the Nazis and Chinese communists — would use this same model in their states. The Russian Revolution resulted in around 10 million deaths; and it became state policy to glorify violence against 'enemies of the revolution'. Other dictators in the 20th century would also emulate *[copy]* this brutality.

C The Russian Revolution also had a significant influence on the two world wars. In late 1917, Russia withdrew from World War One (WWI) due to the revolution. This allowed Germany to move the bulk of its troops from the Eastern Front in Russia to the Western Front in Belgium/France. Although in the end this did not change the outcome of the war, it certainly had the potential to deliver Germany a victory. After WWI, the communist triumph in Russia influenced the policies of governments throughout Europe. This was a contributing factor to the outbreak of World War Two (WWII). During WWII, Russia united with the Western Allies to defeat Nazi Germany. This victory may not have been possible without the massive Russian sacrifice.

D The communist state established by the Russian Revolution continued to influence events even after World War Two. Despite Russia and the West joining in an alliance to defeat Hitler's Germany, a new world order soon appeared. Russia and its other communist allies were on one side, and America and its non-communist allies on the other. This was the so-called Cold War. For over 40 years, the world was under threat of a nuclear war that could destroy civilisation. During this time, both sides attempted to spread their influence elsewhere in the world. This led to smaller but bloody wars in Asia, Africa and South America. New Zealand, like much of the rest of the world, could not escape these influences.

See Chapter 8 onwards for more on topic sentences and paragraph structure in general.

ISBN: 9780170352581

Searching the internet

- Make sure you spell the search terms (words) correctly.
- Be specific — use only the *key words* from the focus question.
- Generally, only use up to FIVE search words/terms: the more words you use, the less focused will be the results that come up.

Key words in the question

- Look at your focus question and underline the key words.
- Usually these key words are one or more of the 5W and 1H: *what, where, why, who, when, how?*

For example: What were the main battles in the Waikato Wars in the 1860s?
'what?' *'what/where?'* *'when?'*

Notice how none of the less important words are included in the search.

A few more search tips

- If you want two or more key terms to both appear together, such as 'Waikato Wars', put them in speech marks as shown. This will bring up only websites that have these two words together, and will ignore the (thousands of) others that have just one or the other.
- If, for some reason, you want to *exclude* some searches from coming up, put a minus sign (-) before the word/term you *don't want* appearing in your searches. For example, if you get a lot of webpages coming up about the Waikato River and for some reason you didn't want these, you could search: 'Waikato Wars -river'

3 ACTIVITY

Identifying key words

Task 1: Underline what you think are the key words in these inquiry focus questions.
Task 2: Put 'speech marks' around any words that you think should be linked together in the search.

a What were the main effects of the Great Depression in 1930s New Zealand?

b What contribution did New Zealand women make at home to the war effort during World War Two?

c Why did French agents bomb the *Rainbow Warrior* in Auckland harbour in 1985?

d What policies in South Africa caused opposition to the 1981 Springbok tour to New Zealand?

e What actions did the Polynesian Panthers take during the 1970s to help Pasifika people in Auckland?

Computer room/own device activity

Try these searches out using the key words that you've identified. Adjust your search terms as necessary to improve your results.

ISBN: 9780170352581

Checking website reading levels

You are probably already aware that the language used in many of the websites you find when doing research is too difficult. There is a relatively easy way to check if a website is easy or hard to understand. Paste the URL of the website you're thinking of using into this website, then click 'Calculate Readability'.

In the example here, this Jewish Virtual Library source has a readability level suitable for 13–14-year-olds. There is additional information and statistics if you are interested. This site may not be perfect, but it will give you an indication of the reading level.

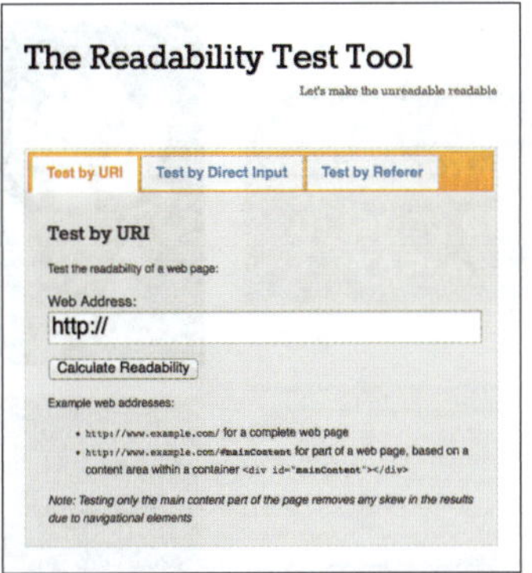

http://read-able.com

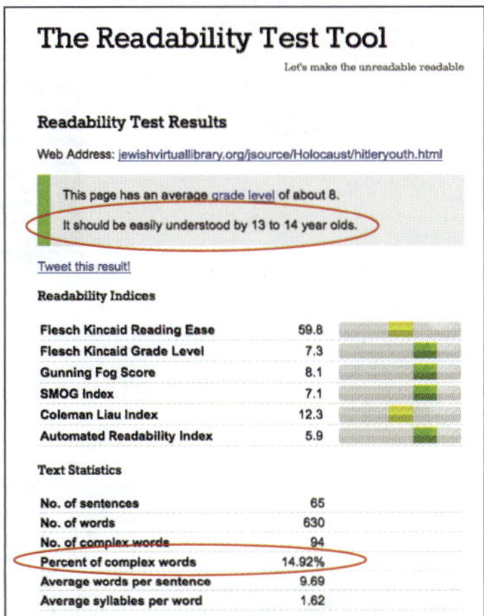

4 ACTIVITY

Try these, noting down the reading age it says for each. Note also the 'Percent of complex words'.

1 http://ww100.govt.nz/

Reading age: ____________ Percent of complex words ____________%

2 http://www.topbusinessentrepreneurs.com/

Reading age: ____________ Percent of complex words ____________%

3 http://www.christchurch.org.nz/Women/

Reading age: ____________ Percent of complex words ____________%

4 http://remember.org/

Reading age: ____________ Percent of complex words ____________%

Some other useful websites

- http://lingro.com/ (makes every word on a website clickable for a dictionary definition).
- http://www.fromtexttospeech.com/ (text-to-speech website that can help with understanding text on a webpage and/or is useful for essay proof-reading).
- http://www.spreeder.com/ (speed-reading assistance).

Quick searching on a webpage

This tip can save you a lot of time and frustration. Apparently, 90 percent of people don't even know about it.

Once you've found a useful-looking website, it can still be hard to find the exact information you want.

- To find a **key word**, on your keyboard press 'CTRL + F' (for a PC) or 'Command + F' (for a Mac). Somewhere on your screen (often near the top), a dialogue box like the one on the next page will appear (this is for a PC).

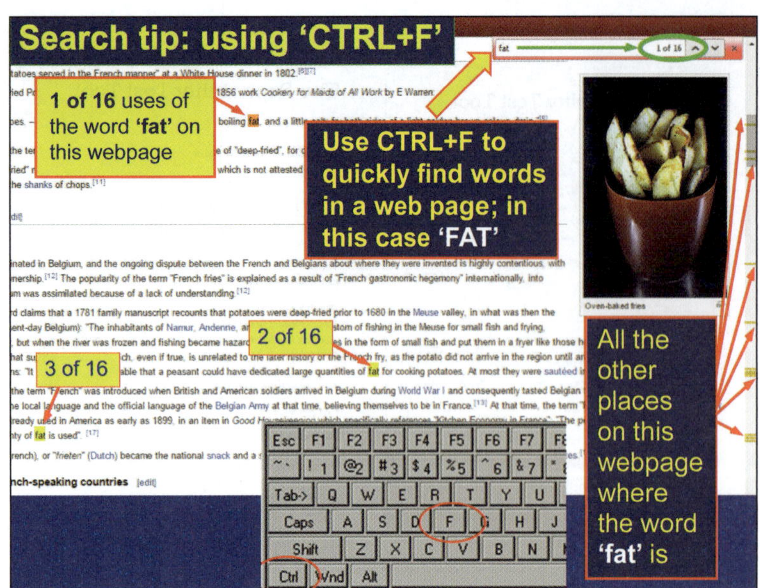

- Type in the key word you want to find (in this example, on a webpage about French fries, it is 'FAT'). All instances of the word 'FAT' will now be highlighted on the webpage. You can use the little arrows (or 'ENTER') to move from one mention of the word 'FAT' to the next.

5 ACTIVITY

Try this in a computer room/on your own device. For this activity, using Wikipedia is simplest.

Search each of the topics below, then do a 'CTRL + F' or 'Command + F' search for the key word(s) given.

Topic	Key word(s)	Number of times it occurs on the page?
Climate change	'greenhouse gas' (or 'greenhouse gases')	
Hitler	'Youth'	
United Nations	'Security Council'	
Vietnam	'ARVN'	
Suffrage	'New Zealand'	

FINISHED?

For each topic, write down brief information from each website about the significance of the key word(s).

Topic	Significance of the key word(s) – *see above*
Climate change	
Hitler	
United Nations	
Vietnam War	
Suffrage	

ISBN: 9780170352581

Using Wikipedia

Wikipedia is around the sixth most frequently visited internet site globally. The main issue with using Wikipedia for an inquiry is not actually to do with reliability (although it can be). Studies have found that the reliability of Wikipedia often compares well with highly regarded publications such as *Encyclopaedia Britannica*, but the fact that articles can be edited by almost anyone can present some problems.

However, more important, as a student of history you need to learn the skills to seek out sources of information for yourself. Wikipedia does indeed offer a lot of information, but someone *else* has done the job of gathering it from a range of different sources. If you are really interested in developing your research skills, then you'll choose not to use Wikipedia — or, at least, to use it as suggested below.

Using Wikipedia 'responsibly'

The main thing to do if using Wikipedia (or similar open sources of information) is to check the article's **references**. These can be found by clicking on the small reference numbers in square brackets that follow pieces of information — for example, the [18] opposite. Clicking on the number will take you to a list of references. These are the sources that the author of the article has used in their own research.

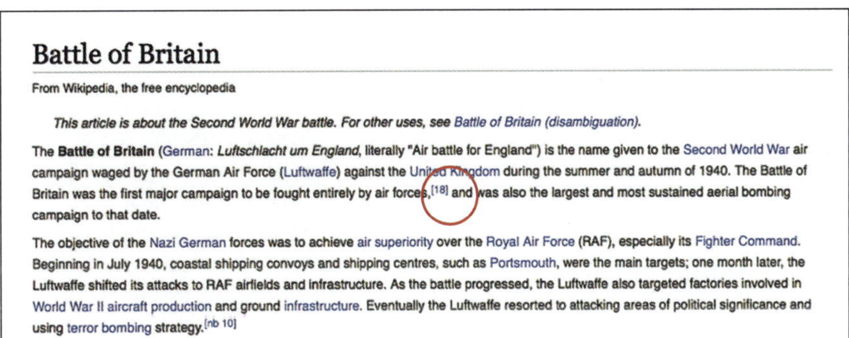

Battle of Britain

From Wikipedia, the free encyclopedia

This article is about the Second World War battle. For other uses, see Battle of Britain (disambiguation).

The **Battle of Britain** (German: *Luftschlacht um England*, literally "Air battle for England") is the name given to the Second World War air campaign waged by the German Air Force (Luftwaffe) against the United Kingdom during the summer and autumn of 1940. The Battle of Britain was the first major campaign to be fought entirely by air forces,[18] and was also the largest and most sustained aerial bombing campaign to that date.

The objective of the Nazi German forces was to achieve air superiority over the Royal Air Force (RAF), especially its Fighter Command. Beginning in July 1940, coastal shipping convoys and shipping centres, such as Portsmouth, were the main targets; one month later, the Luftwaffe shifted its attacks to RAF airfields and infrastructure. As the battle progressed, the Luftwaffe also targeted factories involved in World War II aircraft production and ground infrastructure. Eventually the Luftwaffe resorted to attacking areas of political significance and using terror bombing strategy.[nb 10]

11. ^ a b c d Bungay 2000, p. 368.
12. ^ Ramsay 1989, pp. 251–297.
13. ^ a b "Battle of Britain RAF and FAA Roll of Honour." *RAF*. Retrieved: 14 July 2008.
14. ^ Wood and Dempster 2003, p. 309.
15. ^ Bungay 2000, p. 373.
16. ^ Overy 2001, p. 113.
17. ^ Goodenough 1982, p. 22.
18. ^ "92 Squadron – Geoffrey Wellum." *Battle of Britain Memorial Flight* via *raf.mod.uk*. Retrieved: 17 November 2010.
19. ^ Bungay 2000, pp. 305–306.
20. ^ a b Bungay 2000, p. 388.
21. ^ Stacey 1955, p.18
22. ^ "Battle of Britain - finest hour speech" on Youtube. Retrieved: 1 February 2015.
23. ^ Deighton 1996, pp. 69–73.
24. ^ a b "A Short History of the Royal Air Force," pp. 99–100. *RAF*. Retrieved: 10 July 2011.

Reference number **18**, giving the source of the statement about the Battle of Britain being the first battle entirely fought in the air.

> **Wikipedia tip**
> Instead of using the Wikipedia article for your inquiry, follow the references and use the sources you find there!

Generally speaking, the more references a Wikipedia article has, the better it is likely to be. Having said that, it is still advisable to go further and check the reference itself — this will take you to the original article that the Wikipedia writer has used. You can then make judgments for yourself.

Controversial topics on Wikipedia

Some topics, such as anything to do with the situation in Israel-Palestine, will generate a *lot* of debate. If you were to use information on topics like these direct from Wikipedia, you should check out the 'Talk' and/or 'View history' pages first, by clicking on the appropriate tab at the top of the article. Here you can see the debates among those wishing to make changes to the Wiki page, and how often changes are being made. You can then make your own judgments with regards to reliability — or look elsewhere.

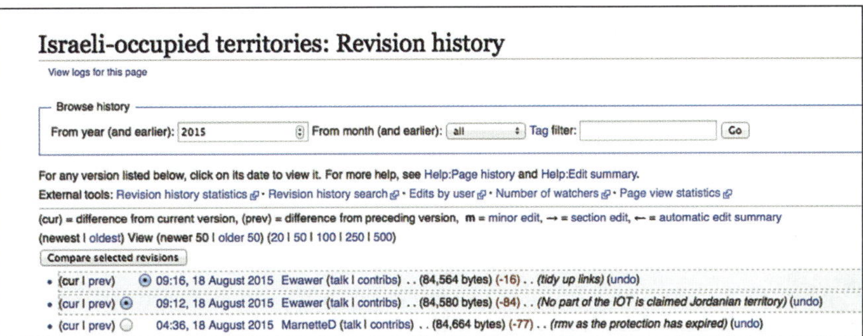

Israeli-occupied territories: Revision history

View logs for this page

Browse history

From year (and earlier): 2015 From month (and earlier): all Tag filter: Go

For any version listed below, click on its date to view it. For more help, see Help:Page history and Help:Edit summary.
External tools: Revision history statistics · Revision history search · Edits by user · Number of watchers · Page view statistics

(cur) = difference from current version, (prev) = difference from preceding version, m = minor edit, → = section edit, ← = automatic edit summary
(newest | oldest) View (newer 50 | older 50) (20 | 50 | 100 | 250 | 500)

Compare selected revisions

- (cur | prev) 09:16, 18 August 2015 Ewawer (talk | contribs) . . (84,564 bytes) (-16) . . *(tidy up links)* (undo)
- (cur | prev) 09:12, 18 August 2015 Ewawer (talk | contribs) . . (84,580 bytes) (-84) . . *(No part of the IOT is claimed Jordanian territory)* (undo)
- (cur | prev) 04:36, 18 August 2015 MarnetteD (talk | contribs) . . (84,664 bytes) (-77) . . *(rmv as the protection has expired)* (undo)

See Chapter 4 for more on how to assess the reliability of websites (and books).

Searching for primary sources

As you might recall, there is in fact an endless supply of primary sources relatively easily available to us all (see pages 4, 6–7). For example, a house (especially an older one) is a primary source, as are the chairs, knives and forks, pictures on the walls and mats on the floor in it! An old soft drink can, video player, car, gravestone, cigarette pack and Scout's badge are also primary sources. Not all of these might be useful, however, for the topics we might wish to explore. Usually, we tend to use written sources and images in our school research, so it is useful to know how to access them, especially online. You can also find a number of original (non-digital) written sources or images at local libraries, museums or other **archives**.

In your web search, add 'primary document' or 'primary source' after your topic.

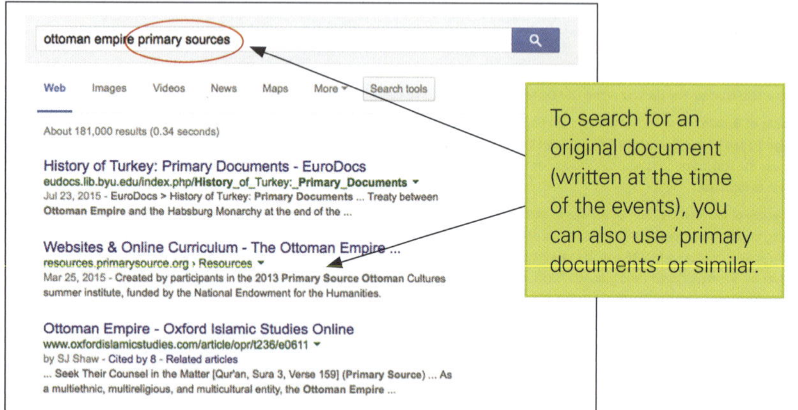

An **archive** (pronounced '*ar*-kive') is a place where old documents and other records are stored. Many businesses, government departments and other organisations have archives. Here is the website of New Zealand's official archive: http://archives.govt.nz/

REFLECTION

1 What is the most useful/interesting thing you have learned from the information about searching?

2 What else would you like to know in terms of carrying out effective book or internet searches?

ISBN: 9780170352581

4 Source reliability

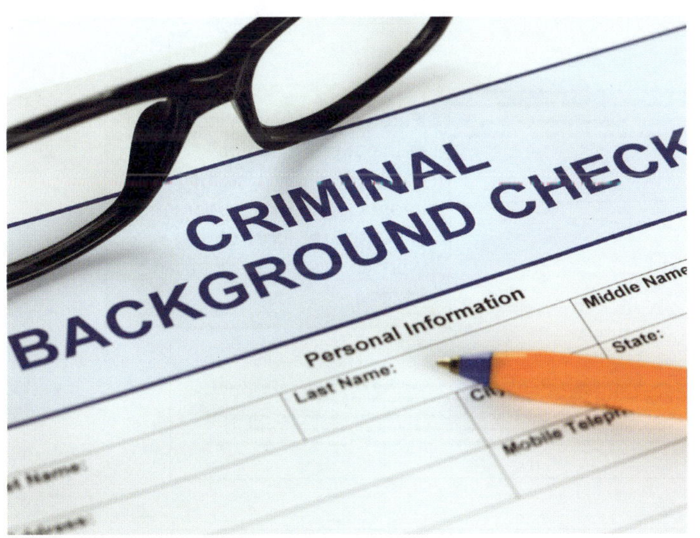

Just like teachers have to have police background checks before they're employed to ensure that they're trustworthy, historians carry out similar 'background checks' on the creators of the sources that they use.

You need to make sure that the sources you use for your inquiry are reliable, whether the sources are books, videos, internet or something else. The best way to do this is to find out about:

- the person (or people) who created the source
- the publishing company or website that made the source available.

Books

- The main test of reliability for books is — just like websites — finding out information on the expertise of the author. Search the author's name online and look for details of their qualifications, as well as the titles of any other books or articles they've published.
- If this doesn't work, or if you'd like to be *really* sure, you can search the name of the **publisher of the book**. Often, universities publish books, which usually makes those books reliable (the reputation of universities depends upon them publishing only quality works). Other large publishing houses also have a reputation to maintain, so wouldn't publish poor-quality works.

ISBN: 9780170352581

In the example here, the author of *Fatal Shore*, a book on Australian history, is Robert Hughes.

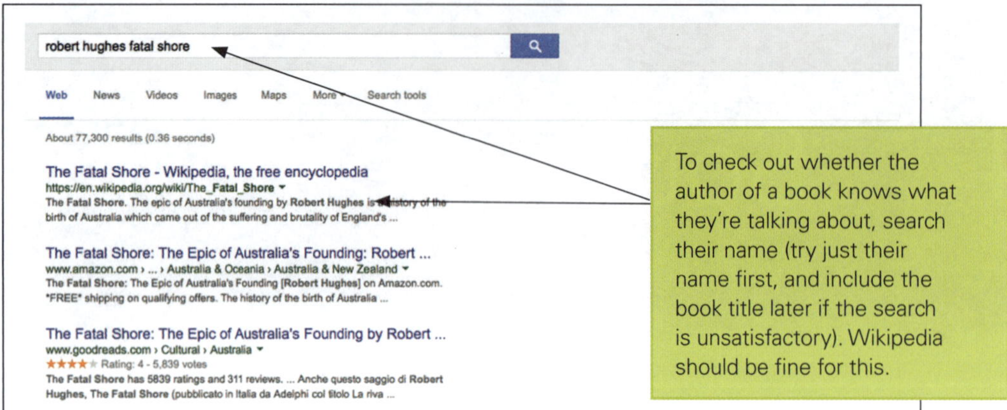

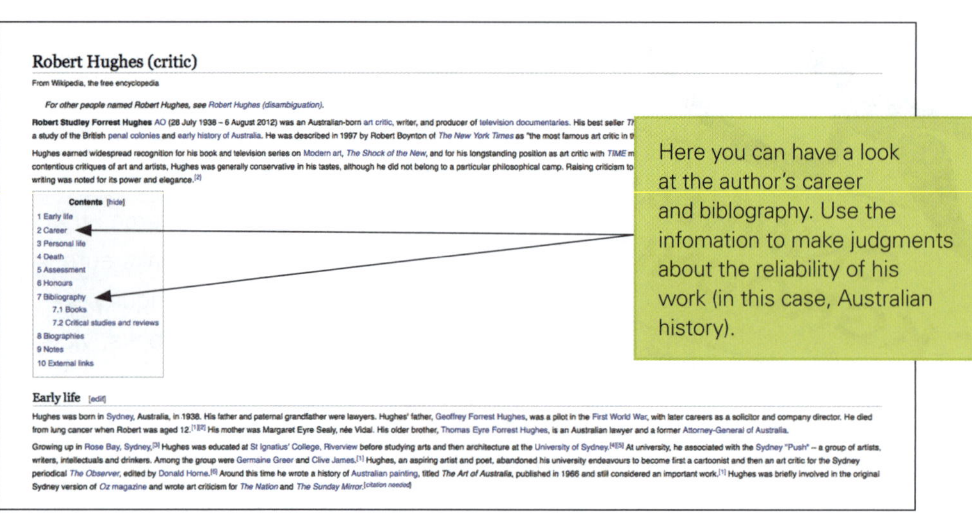

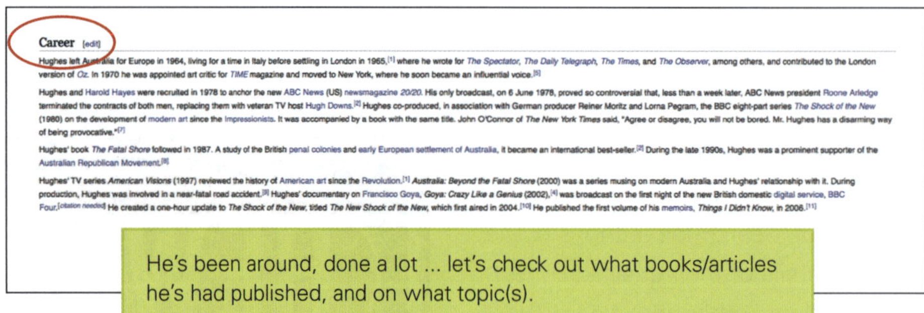

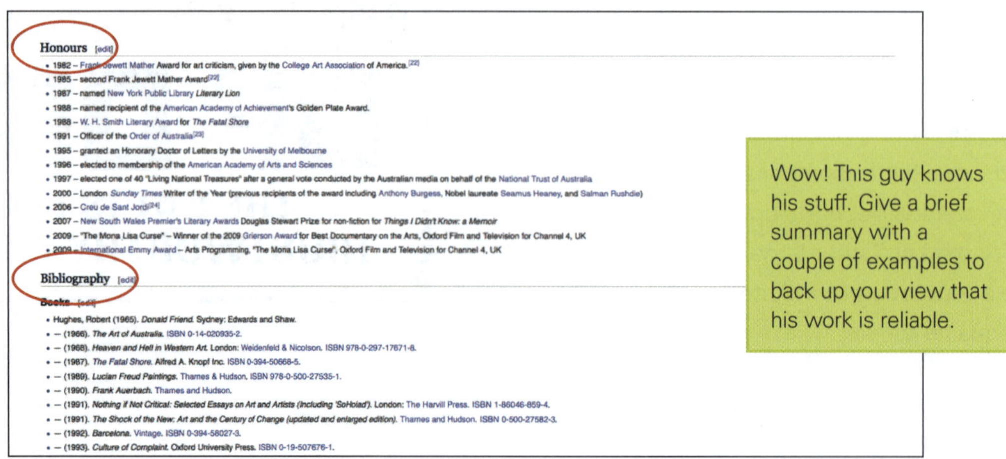

ISBN: 9780170352581

1 ACTIVITY

1 Below is a list of books in which you've found information on a variety of topics. You need to check that the authors are reliable. Fill in the chart below as best you can, commenting on:

- Their education/qualifications, the position they hold (for example, at a university), and for how long.
- Any other relevant books or articles that they've published. Give an example.

2 Find out also some brief details about the **publisher**. The publisher's name is given in brackets after the book title. For example, the publisher of *Making Peoples* by J. Belich is Penguin. You should note down information that shows that the publisher is reputable *[trustworthy]*.

Author/book/publisher	Education/position? (most recent)	Other publications? (most recent)	Publisher information
1 Belich, J. *Making Peoples* (Penguin)			
2 Coney, S. *Standing in the Sunshine* (Viking)			
3 Pugsley, C. *The ANZAC Experience* (Reed Publishing)			
4 Daley, C. *Beauty Queens and Physique Kings* (Auckland University Press)			
5 Harris, A. *Forty Years of Maori Protest* (Huia)			

ISBN: 9780170352581

Summary

Write a two- or three-sentence statement for each book that summarises your findings on both the author and publisher. State whether or not you feel that the source is reliable.

1 ______________________________

2 ______________________________

3 ______________________________

4 ______________________________

5 ______________________________

Library activity

Find three (history) books on any topic of your choice and do a 'background check' on the author AND the publisher. See page 9 for information on how to find the publisher.

1 ______________________________

2 ______________________________

3 ______________________________

Websites

It is much easier and cheaper to publish something on a website than it is to publish in a book, and anyone with a computer and internet connection can do it. This means that any of the three billion or so global internet users could have put up information about the topic that you are researching. Are they all experts on your topic? Unlikely. For this reason, when doing internet-based research, we must take even greater care than we do for books to find out something about the person or organisation that created the information.

ISBN: 9780170352581

There are two fairly easy ways to do this:

1 Most reputable *[trustworthy]* websites have an 'About Us' or 'About the Author' section. There is usually a tab at the very top or very bottom of the page. The 'About Us' section shown here is from Te Ara. As you can see, it gives the qualifications and experience of one of the authors, Malcolm McKinnon.

2 If there is no 'About Us' section, you can search the website name on Wikipedia. (This is another case where Wikipedia can be useful, when used properly.) The example below is for the History Channel. Note that while the History Channel has been around for many years, this report does say that from 2008 the nature of the programmes changed and that it has been criticised by historians and others for screening poorer quality shows. Possibly it would be best *not* to use the History Channel as a source.

Te Ara 'About us'

Malcolm McKinnon is a New Zealand historian. He taught at Victoria University of Wellington 1975–1990 and since 2003 he has also been a writer and theme editor for *Te Ara*, the online encyclopedia of New Zealand. His most well-known work is the *New Zealand Historical Atlas* for which he was the general editor, and which received the 1998 Montana Book Awards Reader's Choice Award. McKinnon is also the author of *Independence and Foreign Policy: New Zealand in the world since 1935*. He was president of the Professional Historians Association of New Zealand/Aotearoa from 2003–2007 and is a vice president of the New Zealand Institute of International Affairs.

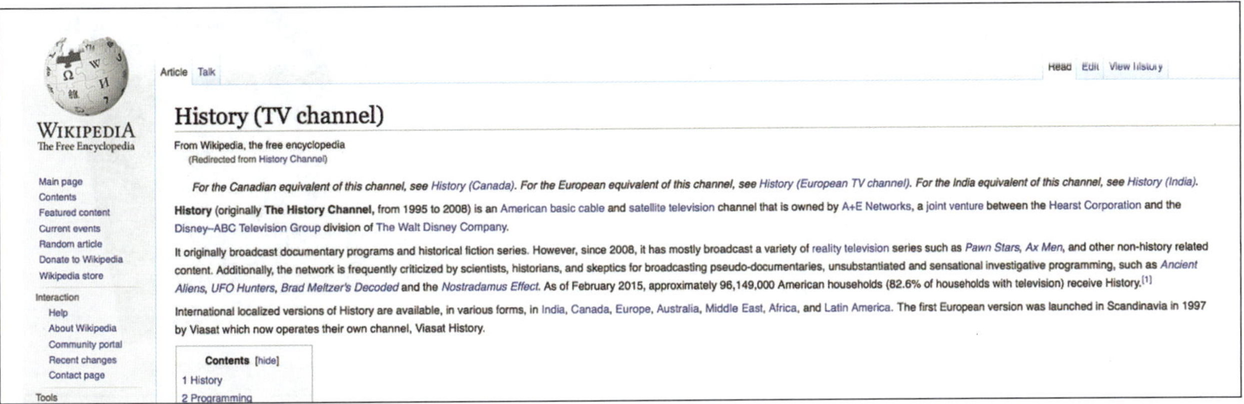

WIKIPEDIA
The Free Encyclopedia

Main page
Contents
Featured content
Current events
Random article
Donate to Wikipedia
Wikipedia store

Interaction
Help
About Wikipedia
Community portal
Recent changes
Contact page

Tools

Article Talk | Read Edit View history

History (TV channel)

From Wikipedia, the free encyclopedia
(Redirected from History Channel)

For the Canadian equivalent of this channel, see History (Canada). For the European equivalent of this channel, see History (European TV channel). For the India equivalent of this channel, see History (India).

History (originally **The History Channel**, from 1995 to 2008) is an American basic cable and satellite television channel that is owned by A+E Networks, a joint venture between the Hearst Corporation and the Disney–ABC Television Group division of The Walt Disney Company.

It originally broadcast documentary programs and historical fiction series. However, since 2008, it has mostly broadcast a variety of reality television series such as *Pawn Stars*, *Ax Men*, and other non-history related content. Additionally, the network is frequently criticized by scientists, historians, and skeptics for broadcasting pseudo-documentaries, unsubstantiated and sensational investigative programming, such as *Ancient Aliens*, *UFO Hunters*, *Brad Meltzer's Decoded* and the *Nostradamus Effect*. As of February 2015, approximately 96,149,000 American households (82.6% of households with television) receive History.[1]

International localized versions of History are available, in various forms, in India, Canada, Europe, Australia, Middle East, Africa, and Latin America. The first European version was launched in Scandinavia in 1997 by Viasat which now operates their own channel, Viasat History.

Contents [hide]
1 History
2 Programming

If you can't find out anything about either the creator of the information on a website, or the organisation that published it, you probably shouldn't use it.

To check the reliability of a source, find out who created it. The first and easiest way is to look in the 'About Us' information tab.

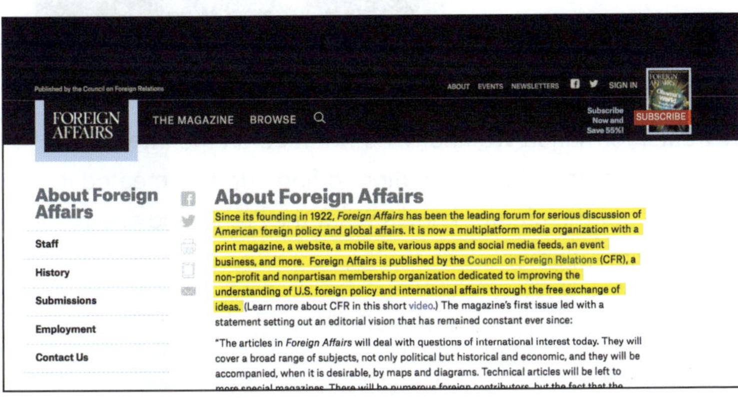

Published by the Council on Foreign Relations

ABOUT EVENTS NEWSLETTERS SIGN IN

FOREIGN AFFAIRS THE MAGAZINE BROWSE

Subscribe Now and Save 55%! SUBSCRIBE

About Foreign Affairs

Staff
History
Submissions
Employment
Contact Us

About Foreign Affairs

Since its founding in 1922, *Foreign Affairs* has been the leading forum for serious discussion of American foreign policy and global affairs. It is now a multiplatform media organization with a print magazine, a website, a mobile site, various apps and social media feeds, an event business, and more. Foreign Affairs is published by the Council on Foreign Relations (CFR), a non-profit and nonpartisan membership organization dedicated to improving the understanding of U.S. foreign policy and international affairs through the free exchange of ideas. (Learn more about CFR in this short video.) The magazine's first issue led with a statement setting out an editorial vision that has remained constant ever since:

"The articles in *Foreign Affairs* will deal with questions of international interest today. They will cover a broad range of subjects, not only political but historical and economic, and they will be accompanied, when it is desirable, by maps and diagrams. Technical articles will be left to

Refer to the criteria on pages 27–28 when you make a comment on source reliability. The 'About' information here suggests this is probably a legitimate site, although its job is to improve 'the understanding of US foreign policy', so will probably give a pro-US view.

Other sources of information

Books and websites are by no means the only places in which to find information useful for an inquiry. Whatever the sources that you do use, you still need to check reliability first.

Historical documentaries

Find out who did the *research* for the documentary. Note that this may not be the same person who presents it on-screen. The researcher should be an historian or other expert. You can also look into the background of the person or company that produced the documentary. If the producer is reputable, then this gives *some* level of assurance that the documentary is reliable. Finally, there may be online reviews that you can check out. Look to see if there are any criticisms of the reliability of the information presented in the documentary. You will need to make your own judgments about whether or not any criticism is justified.

Historical films

While documentaries should be factually based, with plenty of supporting evidence provided, historical films are often more concerned with telling a good story than with being as accurate as possible. In many cases, the bottom line is to make money by entertaining people. This makes most historical films unreliable in terms of being sources for an inquiry.

History magazines or journals

Treat these as you would books. Focus first on the author of the article you're thinking of using, then do some research into the magazine/journal itself. Wikipedia can again be useful for this.

Electronic databases/encyclopaedia

As for any electronic source, don't *assume* that it is reliable because it is found on a reputable database such as EPIC. Look for the creator of the information, or at least find out background information about the specific database.

Secondary source reliability

You understand by now that we cannot simply trust information we find, whether it be on the internet, in books, on TV or anywhere else. We must always 'look behind' the information to find out who created it. Then we need to make a judgment about whether or not the creator knows what they're talking about. On the next page are some criteria for helping us make that judgment.

ISBN: 9780170352581

2 ACTIVITY

What point do you think this cartoonist is making?

The table below gives you some guidance for making decisions about the reliability of secondary sources, based on who created them. Refer to pages 21–22 for guidance on how to find information about the creator of a secondary source.

Criteria for assessing reliability of secondary sources

Creator of the source	Examples of evidence we'd look for regarding the knowledge/skills of the creator of the information/source
Best • Trained historians who are *experts in the <u>particular</u> topic that you are researching.* For example, <u>Tongan</u> history. • Trained historians who are *experts in the <u>general</u> topic that you are researching.* For example, <u>Pasifika</u> history. • A well-known and respected publisher (for books), or news source.	• Name of the university where the degree was earned, and type of degree; position (for example, Professor of History) and how long they've been in it; a list of books or articles they've published; whether or not they've been quoted as a specialist by news organisations, and so on. • Prominent publishers carefully check the works they publish, as their reputation depends on this. This is can also be true of prominent news sources (such as the BBC).
Creator of the source	**Examples of evidence we'd look for regarding the knowledge/skills of the creator of the information/source**
Satisfactory • People who have had training in the historians' skills and use them in their work. This *could* include history teachers, journalists, documentary makers, lawyers or other professionals.	• Name of the university where the degree was earned, and type of degree; position (for example, teacher of history) and how long they've been in it. Any publications or other relevant qualifications.

ISBN: 9780170352581

Other factors that might help convince you that a secondary source is reliable
• It has plenty of **'hard' facts** that can be checked. These could include names (of people, places and events), dates, statistics and/or short quotes. • It has a good number of **references** (notes explaining where the author has found the specific information in a paragraph, or the 'hard' facts provided) and/or a **bibliography** (list of sources used by the author). • The language used by the author is reasonable, without being strongly one-sided or emotive. • More than one viewpoint is presented by the author, even if he or she doesn't agree with them; we are free to make up our own minds based on the evidence presented.

Some final website reliability issues to be aware of

Don't be fooled into thinking a website is reliable *just* from the following.

- It *says* it's reliable, without providing any of the sort of evidence given in the table above.
- It 'looks' good/professional.
- It has had a lot of visits.
- It is owned by a large or well-known company, or one that manages large numbers of well-known websites.
- It has won awards for website *design*.
- It lists genuine-sounding endorsements *[support]* from people who have supposedly used it. *You would need to research who those people were before using this on its own as a reason for trusting the website.*

These are *not* satisfactory reasons (on their own) to accept a website as reliable.

'Hard' facts versus 'soft' facts

Historians always favour the use of 'hard' facts to support their understanding of the past. You should look to use 'hard' facts as often as possible, rather than the alternative 'soft' facts.

A 'soft' fact is similar to a generalisation, or general statement. For example, it is true to say: 'In 1893, there were <u>many</u> New Zealand women who signed a petition demanding the right to vote.' However, 'many' is not a 'hard' (specific) fact.

Here is a 'hard' fact version of this same statement: 'In 1893, there were <u>30,853</u> women who signed a petition demanding the right to vote.'

An acceptable 'hard' fact would also be 'there were nearly 31,000 women who signed ...'.

ISBN: 9780170352581

3 ACTIVITY

Below is information from the 'About Us' sections of some websites that could be used in an inquiry. For each, state whether you think the information on the website would be generally **reliable or not**, and **explain why**.

- Use the criteria from the table on pages 27–28 to guide your decision.
- Highlight **short quotes** from the information below as evidence to back up your decision.

Website 1

Childhood Learning was founded by Jeananda Col and Mitchell Spector in 1993. We began by designing educational games for our own children and in late 1995 started the ChildhoodLearning.com website. We have 25,000 pages on our website covering a wide range of topics. We produce new pages almost every day. Our company's mission is to produce educational materials that emphasize creativity and the pure enjoyment of learning. It has been an amazing adventure for us, and we hope it has been useful for you.

1 Generally reliable? Yes / No / More information needed

2 Explanation of your decision (use the criteria in the table on pages 27–28):

____

____

____

3 Short quote from the source that backs up your decision (highlight it).

Website 2

'Since I began teaching history in England in 1978 I have attempted to produce reliable resources that encourage inter-active learning by students. This has included educational computer programs such as *Attack on the Somme (WWI)* and the *Russian Revolution*. Over the last twenty years I have written over one dozen history books such as *Gandhi* (1987), *Hitler* (1988), *Making of the United Kingdom* (1992), and *The Medieval Village* (1996). My educational qualifications are: Bachelor of Arts, Master of Arts, and Master of Philosophy. In September 1997 I established the Spartacus Educational website and over the next six years I also produced online material for the *Electronic Telegraph*, the European Virtual School and the *Guardian* newspaper's educational website, *Learn*.' — John Simkin

1 Generally reliable? Yes / No / More information needed

2 Explanation of your decision (use the criteria in the table on pages 27–28):

____

____

____

3 Short quote from the source that backs up your decision (highlight it).

ISBN: 9780170352581

Website 3

At AGL, we're in the business of making the Internet better — that's it! Through innovation *[new ideas]* and creativity, we've raised the bar and set the standard for what we believe high quality content is on the Internet. Our content sites and products allow more than 250 million visitors around the world to access the best collection of journalists, artists and musicians on the web. After over 25 years, AGL is still very much a pioneer and we encourage you to come along for the ride and see what's next.

1 Generally reliable? Yes / No / More information needed

2 Explanation of your decision (use the criteria in the table on pages 27–28):

3 Short quote from the source that backs up your decision (highlight it).

Website 4

Our contributing members include war veterans, doctors, librarians, lawyers and students, as well as retirees who have spent their lives absorbing facts and ideas. Whether their answers come from job experience or hobbies, our contributors are eager to channel what they know into a powerful resource, sharing knowledge with hundreds of thousands of people each day. You can contribute, too, if you have the right experience and a desire to spread knowledge to other people.

1 Generally reliable? Yes / No / More information needed

2 Explanation of your decision (use the criteria in the table on pages 27–28):

3 Short quote from the source that backs up your decision (highlight it).

Website 5

John D Clare studied Modern history at Oxford University, and graduated in 1974. He was appointed Head of history in 1979 at Greenfield School, County Durham, where he eventually became Deputy Head Teacher. He was described in the education magazine *Teaching History* as 'the best teacher out there'. He is the author of more than 70 history textbooks, which have been published in 19 countries and 17 different languages. The *I Was There* series included books on *The Pyramids, Ancient Greece, The Roman Empire, The Vikings, Knights in Armour, Medieval Towns, The Italian Renaissance, Christopher Columbus, the Industrial Revolution* and *The First World War.*

1 Generally reliable? Yes / No / More information needed

ISBN: 9780170352581

2 Explanation of your decision (use the criteria in the table on pages 27–28):

3 Short quote from the source that backs up your decision (highlight it).

Discuss your reliability analysis with the rest of the class.

Remember!
Although there are some websites out there that are deliberately fake, we have to take more care with information that is put on websites by non-experts. These could be well-meaning people, but they simply may not know enough about the topic to be reliable.

On the other hand, there are also people out there who are biased — that is, they see things from only *one* point of view and ignore all other views. We have to be sure to consider *all* points of view about an issue, then make our own judgments based on the facts.

4 ACTIVITY

Create an 'About Us' section for an (imaginary) website. You may make it a reliable source of information on a topic of your choice, or not so reliable. (Try not to go for obviously and clearly unreliable — that's too easy.)

Website History topic (of your choice):

'**About Us**' information:

Now, swap them with someone else who will carry out an analysis of the reliability.

Website

1 Generally reliable? Yes / No / More information needed

2 Explanation of your decision (use the criteria in the table on pages 27–28):

3 Short quote from the source that backs up your decision (highlight it).

ISBN: 9780170352581

5 ACTIVITY

When you have access to a computer or other device, locate any two history-based websites (for example, search something like 'Waitangi Tribunal history'). Find the 'About Us' section and note down below the key points that make you feel that the site would be a *reliable* source.

Refer to the 'Criteria for assessing reliability of secondary sources' table on pages 27–28.

Website 1 URL: ______

'**About Us**' key points: ______

Website 2 URL: ______

'**About Us**' key points: ______

REFLECTION

1 What is the most useful/interesting thing you have learned about checking secondary sources for reliability?

2 What else would you like to know in terms of how to check secondary sources for reliability?

 ISBN: 9780170352581

5 Primary source analysis

As noted on page 5, historians use their skills to make sense of the primary sources that they use to write their histories. You've already learned that there are a huge variety of primary sources (see pages 4, 6–7), but we'll focus here on just written and visual sources.

Written sources

There are several key questions any historian will 'ask' of a primary source: these are the very useful '**5W**, **1H**' questions:

1. **Who** created the source?
2. **When** was it created? During what events/issues?
3. **Where** was the person who created it while the events/issues were happening?
4. **Why** did they create it?
5. **What** do other primary sources say about the same event/issue? (Think also about whose voices are missing from the accounts so far.)
6. **How** was the source created?

Note: Written sources mostly give us the views of those who are literate (can read and write). This often leaves large numbers of people out of the historical record, if written sources are the only type used. For example, Maori as a whole were not literate until around the 1830s, even though they have a rich oral (spoken word) history and their carvings and tukutuku panels also tell detailed stories. Elsewhere, in France in the late 17th century the rate of literacy was around 29 percent for men and 14 percent for women. This means we're unlikely to hear directly through written sources from the majority of French people of that time! Fortunately, good historians take this into account and use other methods to 'hear their voices'.

From the answers to these questions, the historian will be able to assess how reliable the source is and take into account any limitations it may have.

1. ***Who* created the source?**

   The most obvious question about a primary source is: Who created it? This question might well have an easy answer if the source is something like a newspaper report, diary entry or (signed) letter. If not, the historian would need to investigate further. Still, just knowing the name of the person who created the source is not really enough: what else can we find out about them? Their job, position, ethnicity and so on — the more information the better!

Official government reports

Except in totalitarian states such as Stalin's Russia or Nazi Germany, for our purposes official government documents such as statistics and other reports should be reliable sources.

ISBN: 9780170352581

2 ***When*** **was the source created?**
What events/issues are happening at the time the source was created? Was the evidence/source created at the time of the events/issues described, or much later?

- If much later (for example, as evidence in a court trial or in the form of an autobiography), is the person's memory of the events reliable? It might well be; Jewish survivors of the Holocaust, for example, remember the events vividly.

In an autobiography, the author *might* emphasise or remember only the positive aspects of their involvement in the events/issues described. It might be, too, that a more entertaining story will sell better than 'the truth', so making money could be at least part of the motivation.

3 ***Where*** **was the person during the events/issues described?**
Was the person directly involved in the events/issues? Perhaps as a participant or a witness, or even as a victim?

- If they were involved, did they have a wide perspective on the event/issue, or was their experience of it 'localised'? If it was localised, other people elsewhere may have had quite different experiences.

Keep in mind that in the past, many people regularly kept diaries or wrote to friends and family elsewhere. Think of this as an earlier form of social media. Plenty of people today are constantly sharing their thoughts online; in the past it was done on paper.

If they were not directly involved, then their evidence is less reliable, but they might still be able to tell us something about the views of other people who were involved.

4 ***Why*** **did the person create the source?**
This is an important question to ask, as it does actually take some degree of effort to write a letter or speech, or to participate in an interview. Why bother doing it?

- The purpose might have been simply to **inform** other people (or themselves, in the case of a diary entry) of the facts about the events/issues. This could be in a letter or report, a statement in a newspaper, table of statistics and so on. *Keep in mind the 'Where?' points noted above.*
- It could have been to **persuade** other people to a certain point of view. If this is the case, we'd need to be careful as other people may have felt quite differently about the same events/issues.
- Taken to its extreme, attempts to persuade in a very one-sided way are called **propaganda**. This is like a type of 'advertising' with the aim of getting people to think or feel a certain way.

Keep in mind that in a private document (for example, a diary or personal letter), the author might be more honest about their views as few other people are intended to see it. In a public document, however, the author will often have thought about how their audience will respond to what they say, and this can in turn influence what is said.

5 ***What*** **do other primary sources say about the same event/issue?**
Historians assemble a 'picture' of the past from the evidence they find. To get the most accurate 'picture' possible they always look for as much relevant primary evidence as they can (see pages 4–7). As more and more sources are found and used, they will help to confirm that the historian is on the right track. If they don't, then the historian will 'change the picture' according to the new evidence and 'throw out' the old version because it is inaccurate. The final version, based on as much supporting evidence as possible, will be published as a history book or article.

Often the '**Where?**' and '**Why?**' questions will require the most thoughtful analysis, and the '**What?**' question is important in terms of the final conclusions an historian will come to about the events/issues in the source(s).

ISBN: 9780170352581

- When looking for additional primary sources, historians will always ask: 'Whose voices are missing from the accounts that I've found so far?' For example, there are many sources written by Pakeha New Zealanders from the 19th century, but fewer by Maori. An historian would soon recognise this imbalance and go looking for sources by Maori in order to get a fuller 'picture of the past'.

Note: For the 'What?' question, the activities that follow will ask you to consider *what other sort of primary sources* you would look for and whose voices are missing from the account. Refer to the activity on pages 6–7 for examples of other primary sources.

6 *How* was the source created?
Many primary sources will have been written by the person themselves, but it is possible that the source might have been written down by somebody else. This could be the case with an interview for a newspaper, journal or a police incident report. It might even be that the person was illiterate (could not read or write) and someone else wrote the information down. This would need to be taken into account when assessing the reliability and/or any possible limitations of the source.

Newspapers

Newspapers generally 'report the truth' — as they see it — but the 'whole truth' may not be immediately clear at the time. Newspaper reports are sometimes called 'the first draft of history'. Historians will use them but also look for other sources as well. Like historians we need to be cautious, as even newspapers tend to have particular points of view. It is important to recognise that they often reflect the values of:

- the times in which they are published. For example, during the 1960s it was completely normal for women to be in the home as mothers and wives, and newspaper articles and advertisements reflected and reinforced those roles.
- those who *own* the newspaper. Although many newspaper owners allow their editor and journalists to report the news without interference, ultimately the owner has the power to enforce their view if they wish.
- businesses/people that *advertise* in the paper. Advertising is the main income source for most newspapers (especially in pre-digital times). If a newspaper continually takes a position on one or more issues that the advertisers do not like, then they may withdraw their business. This can be damaging to the newspaper if the amount of lost income is significant.
- those who buy and *read* it. While in New Zealand the population is too small for a wide range of newspapers to exist, in places like Britain the newspapers tend to target specific sections of society (see the table below). This is generally quite well known, so an historian using these as a source would take that into account during their analysis.

Examples of the political views of some British newspapers

Title	Political viewpoint
The Daily Telegraph	Right, conservative
Financial Times	Economically liberal, politically centrist
The Sunday Times	Right, conservative
The Guardian	Centre-left and social-liberal
The Independent	Economically liberal, politically centre-left
The Times	Centre-right

Here are some British newspaper headlines reporting the death of former Prime Minister Margaret Thatcher. She became widely known as the 'Iron Lady' due to her strong policies that dramatically changed British society. Some say that she saved Britain, while others say that she destroyed it. Clearly, as an historian it would be important to understand the political position of each newspaper when using it as a source of information.

Socialist Worker
REJOICE!
THATCHER'S DEAD SPECIAL PULL OUT

DAILY Mirror
MARGARET THATCHER DEAD AT 87
The woman who divided a nation

THE SCOTSMAN
MARGARET THATCHER 1925-2013
'Patriot Prime Minister' who divided the nation

NEWSPAPER OF THE YEAR
20p
i
The essential daily briefing
Thatcher
As divisive in death as she was in life

Daily Mail
The woman who saved Britain
1925-2013
SPECIAL TRIBUTE EDITION

10p DAILY EXPRESS
Margaret Thatcher dies, aged 87, after suffering a stroke
'We've lost a great leader and a great Briton'
UNIQUE PULLOUT INSIDE
SPECIAL COMMEMORATIVE EDITION
FAREWELL IRON LADY

The Star
'WE CAN NEVER FORGIVE HER'
Foster Carers needed

All of the sources in activities 1 – 5 have been typed up from the original documents, some of which were handwritten while others were printed texts.

1 ACTIVITY

Refer to the source below and, as best you can, answer these '5W, 1H' analysis questions (see pages 33–35).

Dec. 8th 1859
Windsor, Augusta County
Virginia, USA

Dear Children

I am seated trying to write a few lines to Let you no how we get along this stormy Sabbath evening I have Been to Church to day not many there but there was a funeral. Sermon to Be preached on the Death of a Mrs Simons a taylor in the village she went to Delhi on a visit and died there. Mr Copley has lost three Children with the Scarlet fever.

You speak of excitement and Commotion [the possibility of war] But I think you need have no fears from the folks here in the North; we do not wish to interfere with you on slavery. Personally, I had rather work myself than have slaves. We know there is some that would like to stir up political trouble But if you at the South feel it is aproved by god to have slaves then all is well I wish you to have the smiles and approbation *[approval]* of a holy god who does all thing right and to whome we must all stand or fall for ourselves. Look at the matter Candidly *[honestly]* and impartially *[neutrally]* — if we have peace within ourselves then the storm outside will not disturb us.

Your affectionate mother

Lydia Hotchkiss

Write soon!

ISBN: 9780170352581

1 **Who** created the source? *Give more details than just the name.* ______________________________

____

2 **When** was it created? (During what events/issue?) ______________________________

____

3 **Where** was the person who created it while the events/issues were happening? ______________________________

____

4 **Why** did they create it? ______________________________

____

5 **What** additional primary sources would you try to find to see whether or not the information in this source is part of a 'bigger picture'? *Whose voices, missing from the account below, would you also try to find?* ______________________________

____

6 **How** was the source created? ______________________________

Summarise your analysis here.

Strengths of the source	Any weaknesses/limitations of the source
Overall comment on reliability of this source in terms of the events described:	

TODAY IN HISTORY

MARCH

1/3/1692	The Salem (Massachussets) witch trials begin. Over a few months of hysteria 19 people are executed as witches.
5/3/1953	Death of Josef Stalin aged 73, after 29 years in power.
9/3/1939	Barbie Doll retails for the first time
10/3/1876	Alexander Graham Bell makes first telephone call, to his assistant in the next room: 'Mr Watson, come here, I want you.'
22/3/1848	First settlers arrive at Dunedin
26/3/1942	Jews first sent to Auschwitz concentration camp in Poland

2 ACTIVITY

Refer to the source below and, as best you can, answer these '5W, 1H' analysis questions.

'An address *[speech]* to the Loyal Citizens and Congress *['parliament']* of the United States of America presented by a convention *[meeting]* of Negroes held in Alexandria, Virginia, from August 2 to 5, 1865'

Well, the civil war is over and we Negroes are declared free from the chains of slavery! Yet four fifths of our enemies have already been set free without punishment, and the other fifth are in the process of being pardoned! The President has, in his efforts at recovery of the southern States, left us entirely at the mercy of these defeated but unapologetic rebels. We might just as well be slaves again, so much of the power has been given back to them. We know these men — know them well — and we assure you that, with the majority of them, loyalty is only 'lip deep'; by all sorts of unfriendly local legislation *[laws]* they will make the freedom the government has given us more intolerable *[unbearable]* than slavery. In one word, the only salvation *[rescue]* for us is in the possession of the right to vote. Give us this, and we Negroes will protect ourselves …'

1 **Who** created the source? ____________________

____

2 **When** was it created? (During what events/issue?) ____________________

____

3 **Where** was the person who created it while the events/issues were happening? ____________________

____

4 **Why** did they create it? ____________________

____

5 **What** additional primary sources would you try to find to see whether or not the information in this source is part of a 'bigger picture'? *Whose voices, missing from the account below, would you also try to find?* ____________________

____

6 **How** was the source created? ____________________

Summarise your analysis here.

Strengths of the source	Any weaknesses/limitations of the source

Overall comment on reliability of this source in terms of the events described:

ISBN: 9780170352581

3 ACTIVITY

Refer to the source below and, as best you can, answer these '5W, 1H' analysis questions.

> Twice in our region there was an earthquake; the first in the night following Palm Sunday, the second in the holy night of Christ's resurrection *[Easter]* in the Year of our Lord eight hundred and forty-five. In this same year the heathen *[non-Christian]* Vikings broke in upon the Christians at many points, but more than twelve thousand of the Vikings were killed by our neighbours the Frisians *[Western Germans]*. Another party of invaders devastated Gaul *[southern France]*; of these more than six hundred men perished. Yet owing to his indolence *[laziness]*, King Charles agreed to give them many thousands of pounds of gold and silver if they would leave Gaul, and this they did. Nevertheless the cloisters *[chapels]* of most of the saints were destroyed, and many of the Christians were led away captive into slavery. We can only thank God that they left Xanten Abbey *[monastery]* alone, but one does wonder for how long we will be safe from these wild men. This finishes my report for this dreadful year.

1 **Who** created the source? ______________________

____

2 **When** was it created? (During what events/issue?) ______________________

____

3 **Where** was the person who created it while the events/issues were happening? ______________________

____

4 **Why** did they create it? ______________________

____

5 **What** additional primary sources would you try to find to see whether or not the information in this source is part of a 'bigger picture'? *Whose voices, missing from the account below, would you also try to find?* ______________________

____

6 **How** was the source created? ______________________

Summarise your analysis here.

Strengths of the source	Any weaknesses/limitations of the source

ISBN: 9780170352581

Overall comment on reliability of this source in terms of the events described:

4 ACTIVITY

Refer to the source below and, as best you can, answer these '5W, 1H' analysis questions.

'In August 1945, when I was 16, the Western Allies marched into Berlin and the city was divided up. My mother and I lived in Neukölln, in the American sector. We were very happy about this — the Americans gave us food and slowly life became more bearable again. But it was not to last. Soviet Russia's leader Stalin started acting badly towards the Allies, reaching its height in the complete blockade *[sealing off]* of West Berlin as of June 24, 1948. Every over-land access route was blocked and the supply routes of the British, French and American sectors were cut off. Stalin's aim was to force the Western powers to retreat and to place Berlin under his Communist control. It was a prospect *[possibility]* that terrified us: We could not imagine anything worse — to fall into the hands of the Russians, who we had encountered when Berlin had fallen three years earlier. All our hopes now rested on the Allies.

And they didn't let us down. Only 48 hours after the city had been cut off from the world, the Allies flew the first plane into Berlin to supply the city with essentials — the beginning of an airlift that would end up lasting over a year. Despite threats from the Soviets, the Americans and the Brits kept at it, supplying us with food and coal through three flight routes. Every three minutes a plane landed at Tempelhof airport and several planes were always in the sky overhead. These pilots and men risked their lives for us — and that despite the fact that we Germans had been their enemies in the war and had killed many of their countrymen. It was clear to us in Berlin that if the Americans could defy the Russians, we also had to get through this, even though it was really tough at times. You young people today forget what the Americans and British did for us; I may be old and nearly at the end of my life but I want you to remember this lesson. Thank you for listening.'

1 **Who** created the source? ______________________

2 **When** was it created? (During what events/issue?) ______________________

3 **Where** was the person who created it while the events/issues were happening? ______________________

4 **Why** did they create it? ______________________

ISBN: 9780170352581

5 **What** additional primary sources would you try to find to see whether or not the information in this source is part of a 'bigger picture'? *Whose voices, missing from the account below, would you also try to find?* ______________________________________

6 **How** was the source created? ______________________________

Summarise your analysis here.

Strengths of the source	Any weaknesses/limitations of the source
Overall comment on reliability of this source in terms of the events described:	

5 ACTIVITY

Refer to the source below and, as best you can, answer these '5W, 1H' analysis questions.

From: 2335 Norwalk Avenue
Los Angeles 41, Calif.
September 12, 1948

To: President Harry S. Truman,
1600 Pennsylvania Avenue,
Washington D.C.

Dear Sir

The so-called 'Berlin Crisis' is entirely an outgrowth of your own incredible stupidity. When you attended the Potsdam Conference to arrange final details for the occupation of Germany [near the end of WWII], it was your duty to look out for American interests and insist upon the establishment of a corridor to the American Zone of Berlin, for ingress and egress *[in and out traffic]* to the city. This you failed to do. Possibly this was because you believed *[Soviet leader]* Joseph Stalin to be a 'good old chap', as you expressed it some time ago. But I am inclined to think that you were just too dumb to know that such a corridor was necessary.

In the meantime, you seem to be willing and even eager to force this country into a war with Russia merely for the purpose of 'saving face'. If you do this, the blame for such a war will rest upon your own shoulders, and the blood of American boys butchered in this war will be on your head. Read the enclosed article from the Los Angeles Times of September 12, and then perhaps even your feeble mind will grasp the fact that the Berlin Crisis can be solved without dragging the United States into war.

Yours truly

PHILLIP JOHNSTON

ISBN: 9780170352581

1 **Who** created the source? ______________________

____

2 **When** was it created? (During what events/issue?) ______________________

____

3 **Where** was the person who created it while the events/issues were happening? ______________________

____

4 **Why** did they create it? ______________________

____

5 **What** additional primary sources would you try to find to see whether or not the information in this source is part of a 'bigger picture'? *Whose voices, missing from the account below, would you also try to find?* ______________________

____

6 **How** was the source created? ______________________

Summarise your analysis here.

Strengths of the source	Any weaknesses/limitations of the source
Overall comment on reliability of this source in terms of the events described:	

TODAY IN HISTORY

APRIL

10/4/1633 Bananas go on sale in England for the first time
15/4/1955 McDonald's founded by Ray Kroc in Chicago
21/4/1918 German WWI air ace Baron Manfred von Richthofen (the 'Red Baron') killed in action
25/4/1945 Delegates of 45 nations meet in San Francisco to organise the United Nations
30/4/1945 Hitler commits suicide and his remains are partially cremated

ISBN: 9780170352581

ADDITIONAL ACTIVITY

Create ONE primary source of your own in the space below. It can be about any historical topic. Use the '5W, 1H' questions from the previous activities to guide you. You will need to include the answers to most or all of these questions somewhere within your source.

When you have finished, swap your work with someone else and have them complete the analysis questions.

Your 'created' primary source

Analysis activity

(Get a classmate to complete this.)

Refer to the source above and, as best you can, answer these '5W, 1H' analysis questions.

1 **Who** created the source?

2 **When** was it created? (During what events/issue?)

3 **Where** was the person who created it while the events/issues were happening?

4 **Why** did they create it?

5 **What** additional primary sources would you try to find to see whether or not the information in this source is part of a 'bigger picture'? *Whose voices, missing from the account below, would you also try to find?*

6 **How** was the source created?

Summarise your analysis here.

Strengths of the source	Any weaknesses/limitations of the source
Overall comment on reliability of this source in terms of the events described:	

Visual sources

The same useful '**5W**, **1H**' questions an historian would ask of a written source can be asked of a visual one, such as a photograph or painting/drawing.

You may not be able to answer all of these 5W, 1H questions, but even thinking carefully about them means that you will be engaging more with the source.

1 **Who** created the source?
2 **When** was it created?
3 **Where** was the person who created it while the events/issues were happening?
4 **Why** did they create it?
5 **What** do other primary sources (of any sort) say about the same event/issue?
6 **How** was the source created?

 ISBN: 9780170352581

Note: Analysis of images is always much easier if they come with a caption. If they do, use that information; if they don't, the historian must become much more of a detective!

Photography was mostly limited to professionals until the introduction of the 'Box Brownie' camera in 1900. Even then, it was still a very expensive hobby. By 1955, the cost of buying and developing a roll of film (eight pictures) was about $15 in today's money, nearly $2 for each photograph!

1 ***Who* created the image?**

While it might seem that a photograph is quite different to a painting or drawing, they all have similarities when it comes to the 'Who?' question. Both the photographer and the artist can set up the way the subject of their work is to be captured, whether that be on film or on canvas/paper. They often choose what to include in the image and what to leave out. Knowing something about who created the image can help the historian accurately analyse it.

- As with written sources, which capture mostly the experiences of those who are literate, those who are not particularly artistic or don't have easy access to a camera may not leave much of a visual record of their experiences.

2 ***When* was the image created?**

What events/issues are happening at the time the image was created? Was the image captured at the time of these events/issues, or much later? A photograph would usually be taken at the time, but it *could* possibly be a reconstruction done later. An artwork could be done at the time and/or at a later date from memory. How much later could affect the reliability of the source.

An additional point to consider with photography is that the older the technology, the more the photographer had to 'stage manage' the photo. This is because in the 19th century, the subjects of photos had to remain completely still for quite some time so that the image would not be blurred.

3 ***Where* was the person who captured the events/issues as an image?**

As for written sources, the photographer or artist might find it difficult to be everywhere and see everything in order to record it. Because of this, they might have only a narrow understanding of the events/issues from what they experienced of them. It is important to keep in mind that other people elsewhere may have had a very different experience. The historian would, of course, try to find records of these different experiences.

- Paintings from earlier times of significant historical events, such as Captain Cook's death in Hawaii in 1779, were often done by artists back in Europe from accounts that they had read! Such images are not very reliable in terms of learning more about the event itself.

4 ***Why* did the person create the image?**

Once again we must ask: Why did the person bother creating the image? While it is extremely easy and cheap today to take photographs, it wasn't always the case. A drawing takes some time to do and a painting even longer (these were really the only ways to capture images in the days before photography).

ISBN. 9780170352581

- As with written sources, the purpose might have been simply to **inform/ keep a record of events** for other people or themselves. This could be for public viewing, such as in a newspaper, newsreel or magazine. If they are personal, such images might remain within a household on the wall or in a photo album (or, more recently, online).
- Images are a powerful form of media, so are often used to **persuade** other people to a certain point of view. If this is the case, the photographer or artist will intentionally capture the image in a certain way.
- As we already know, taken to its extreme, attempts to persuade in a very one-sided way are called **propaganda**. Images are excellent for this as they can communicate a powerful message without the need for too many words.

Because of the limitations of older photographic technology and the relatively high cost, it was not uncommon for the person paying for the image to have it posed to show a particular version of their lives. This isn't so different to everyone suddenly putting on big smiles when a camera is pointed their way today.

5 *What* do other primary sources say about the same event/issue?

As with written or any other types of primary sources, the historian will always ensure that they have as wide a range as possible before coming to any conclusions.

- The activities that follow will ask you to consider *what other sort of primary sources* you would look for and *whose experiences of the event/issue are missing*. Refer to the activities on pages 6–7 for examples of other primary sources.

6 *How* was the source created?

- While **paintings, drawings and sketches** can be done while events are happening, they cannot capture those events as quickly as a photograph. This means that they often capture the *impression* that the events left on the artist. Portraits, where the subject sits for them, or relatively still scenes (such as a farm or forest) can be quite accurate, although will still reflect the artist's style and training.
- With **photographs**, there are essentially two key questions to ask: Is the image 'natural' or is it 'posed'/'stage-managed'? With a posed photograph, the photographer (or the person paying the photographer) wants a certain version of events to be recorded (think of the calls to 'smile' before a group photograph). The historian will take this into account when analysing such a source. However, even if the image is 'natural', the photographer still makes a decision about what to include and what to exclude in the frame. Even the angle (for example, high or low) and the lighting settings can influence how the photograph looks.

It is true that photographs can be 'doctored' or altered, even pre-digital ones; however, this is not actually very common. Much more common is to 'stage manage' photos so that they show what the photographer (or the person paying the photographer) wants.

ISBN: 9780170352581

ACTIVITY EXAMPLE

Refer to the image below and, as best you can, answer these '5W, 1H' analysis questions.

Sister Pretty departing — a Boer [South African] war nurse, around 1900.

1 **Who** do you think might have created the image? Perhaps a journalist or professional photographer.

2 **When** was it created? (During what event/issue? Describe this as best you can, based on what you can see.) Just looking at the photo, it looks like it's quite old, given the dresses that the women are wearing and the fact that there are horses and a wagon. The man with the women might be wearing a military uniform, so possibly it's during a war or training for a war. The wagon has a (red?) cross on it so is probably an ambulance. Now looking at the caption, it is indeed an old photograph (around 1900) and the event is the Boer [South African] War. Judging by the long shadows, it is early morning or late afternoon.

3 **Where** was the person who created it while the event/issue was happening? The photograph seems to have been taken in quite an empty space so perhaps the photographer had to come with the group to photograph them? It's hard to know if anything more is going on outside of this photo. It's also hard to know where exactly Sister Pretty is departing from, as per the caption. She might well be going to a hospital nearer the actual battles.

4 **Why** do you think the person created it? It doesn't seem like this would be very useful for propaganda, so it might just be to keep a record of this event. Perhaps it is to show the role of women in this conflict, or perhaps it is just a friend or the nursing organisation she belongs to recording the event.

5 **What** additional primary sources would you try to find to see whether or not the information in this source is part of a 'bigger picture'? *Whose experiences of this event/issue, missing from the image below, might you also try to find?* More photographs by this photographer would be useful; so would some newspaper reports from the time. Possibly Sister Pretty or one of the people in the photo kept a diary, so that would be very useful. There will also no doubt be official reports on the war, so military records on the role of nurses would be worth finding. Perhaps we could even find a list

ISBN: 9780170352581

of the nursing supplies sent to the conflict, like those in the back of the wagon; this would tell us something about medical care at the time.

6 **How** was the source created? It is an old photograph and, as it says in the 'How?' information above, the old technology might mean that the people in this photo had to hold their pose for a while. In this case, the photo would tell us a bit more about the image that the people in it (and/or the photographer) want us to see.

Summarise your analysis here.

Usefulness of the source	Any weaknesses/limitations of the source
There is a caption, so we have that information. We know when (approximately) this photo was taken and that Sister Pretty was 'important' enough to have her photo taken and her name (alone) recorded. We can see the clothing and technology of the time (horse and wagon for transport). It also tells us that women were involved in this conflict (at least as nurses). The landscape is rather bare, so might suggest the conditions in which the fighting took place.	As always, one source is not enough to make too many solid claims about the past; we would need to find many more. We don't know who the photographer was, or for certain what the purpose of the photo was; nor do we know more than this was somewhere in South Africa, presumably near to the conflict itself.

6 ACTIVITY

Image 1

Refer to the image below and, as best you can, answer these '5W, 1H' analysis questions. Note: with the clues you have from these images, you may research further online to give depth to your response.

Washington, USA, 1963.

ISBN: 9780170352581

1 **Who** do you think might have created the image?

2 **When** was it created? (During what event/issue? Describe this as best you can, based on what you can see.)

3 **Where** was the person who created it while the event/issue was happening?

4 **Why** do you think the person created it?

5 **What** additional primary sources would you try to find to see whether or not the information in this source is part of a 'bigger picture'? *Whose experiences of this event/issue, missing from the image below, might you also try to find?*

6 **How** was the source created?

Summarise your analysis here.

Usefulness of the source	Any weaknesses/limitations of the source

TODAY IN HISTORY

MAY

8/5/1863 Dunedin's streets are the first to be lit by gas lighting.

20/5/1874 Levi Strauss markets blue denim jeans with copper rivets, $13.50 a dozen

23/5/1966 Piki Paki, daughter of King Koroki, becomes Maori Queen Te Atairangikaahu on the death of her father

28/5/1965 NZ joins Vietnam War with an announcement by Keith Holyoake that an artillery unit will be sent

29/5/1953 Hillary and Tensing Norgay reach the summit of Mt Everest

31/5/1886 A tourist party on Lake Tarawera report seeing a ghostly waka, later considered an omen when Tarawera erupts

ISBN: 9780170352581

7 ACTIVITY

Image 2

Refer to the image below and, as best you can, answer these '5W, 1H' analysis questions. Note: with the clues you have from these images, you may research further online to give depth to your response.

Infantry in action, 1917.

1 **Who** do you think might have created the image?

____

2 **When** was it created? (During what event/issue? Describe this as best you can, based on what you can see.) ______________________________

____

____

3 **Where** was the person who created it while the event/issue was happening?

____

4 **Why** do you think the person created it? ______________________________

____

5 **What** additional primary sources would you try to find to see whether or not the information in this source is part of a 'bigger picture'? *Whose experiences of this event/issue, missing from the image below, might you also try to find?*

____

____

ISBN: 9780170352581

6 **How** was the source created?

Summarise your analysis here.

Usefulness of the source	Any weaknesses/limitations of the source

8 ACTIVITY

Image 3

Refer to the image below and, as best you can, answer these '5W, 1H' analysis questions. Note: with the clues you have from these images, you may research further online to give depth to your response.

East Cleveland, USA.

1 **Who** do you think might have created the image?

2 **When** was it created? (During what event/issue? Describe this as best you can, based on what you can see.) ______

______

______

3 **Where** was the person who created it while the event/issue was happening?

______

4 **Why** do you think the person created it? ______

______

5 **What** additional primary sources would you try to find to see whether or not the information in this source is part of a 'bigger picture'? *Whose experiences of this event/issue, missing from the image below, might you also try to find?*

______

______

6 **How** was the source created? ______

______

Summarise your analysis here.

Usefulness of the source	Any weaknesses/limitations of the source

TODAY IN HISTORY

JUNE

2/6/1858	Potatau Te Wherowhero accepted the role of first Maori King
3/6/1896	Henry Ford takes his first car for a trial run
6/6/1944	D-Day invasion of Allied troops at German-held Normandy (France)
8/6/1965	President Johnson authorises the use of US combat troops in Vietnam. Troop numbers peaked in 1969 at 500,000.
10/6/1793	First public zoo, Le Jardin des Plantes, opens in Paris
11/6/1901	The Cook Islands and Niue are annexed to New Zealand
17/6/1885	The Statue of Liberty arrives in New York City aboard the French ship *Isere* in 214 crates
27/6/1902	New Zealand flag officially adopted
29/6/1950	New Zealand joins the Korean War

ISBN: 9780170352581

9 ACTIVITY

Image 4

Refer to the image below and, as best you can, answer these '5W, 1H' analysis questions. Note: with the clues you have from these images, you may research further online to give depth to your response.

Anti-Springbok [South African rugby team] Tour, Dunedin 1981. Note: apartheid was a policy of the South African government that racially separated blacks and whites.

1 **Who** do you think might have created the image?

____

2 **When** was it created? (During what event/issue? Describe this as best you can, based on what you can see.) ______________________________

____

____

3 **Where** was the person who created it while the event/issue was happening?

____

4 **Why** do you think the person created it? ______________________________

____

5 **What** additional primary sources would you try to find to see whether or not the information in this source is part of a 'bigger picture'? *Whose experiences of this event/issue, missing from the image below, might you also try to find?*

____

____

6 **How** was the source created?

Summarise your analysis here.

Usefulness of the source	Any weaknesses/limitations of the source

10 ACTIVITY

Image 5

Refer to the image below and, as best you can, answer these '5W, 1H' analysis questions. Note: with the clues you have from these images, you may research further online to give depth to your response.

Queenstown, 1878.

1 **Who** do you think might have created the image?

2 **When** was it created? (During what event/issue? Describe this as best you can, based on what you can see.)

 ISBN: 9780170352581

3 **Where** was the person who created it while the event/issue was happening?

4 **Why** do you think the person created it?

5 **What** additional primary sources would you try to find to see whether or not the information in this source is part of a 'bigger picture'? *Whose experiences of this event/issue, missing from the image below, might you also try to find?*

6 **How** was the source created?

Summarise your analysis here.

Usefulness of the source	Any weaknesses/limitations of the source

11 ACTIVITY

Image 6

Refer to the image below and, as best you can, answer these '5W, 1H' analysis questions. Note: with the clues you have from these images, you may research further online to give depth to your response.

Cape Helles (Gallipoli), May 1915.

ISBN: 9780170352581

1 **Who** do you think might have created the image?

2 **When** was it created? (During what event/issue? Describe this as best you can, based on what you can see.)

3 **Where** was the person who created it while the event/issue was happening?

4 **Why** do you think the person created it?

5 **What** additional primary sources would you try to find to see whether or not the information in this source is part of a 'bigger picture'? *Whose experiences of this event/issue, missing from the image below, might you also try to find?*

6 **How** was the source created?

Summarise your analysis here.

Usefulness of the source	Any weaknesses/limitations of the source

Altered images

While you usually won't have to deal in your school studies with historical images that have been altered, it is worthwhile noting that there have been a number of instances of this occurring in the past (and many cases of it occurring in more recent times, especially with the development of digital technology). You can use search terms such as 'altered historical images' to find further examples on the internet.

The series of photos (top of next page) shows how Soviet leader Joseph Stalin (the sole 'survivor' in the last photograph) erased his former colleagues from the photographic record after they fell out of favour.

In the first photograph, Ivan Akulov stands to the right of Stalin. Akulov had been involved in the efforts to overthrow the Russian Tsar (Emperor) as early as 1913, and had joined in the 1917 Revolution on the same side as Stalin. By 1937 he had risen to a top position in the Communist Party. Stalin, however, had become increasingly paranoid about supposed threats to his authority and, in July 1937, Akulov became another high-ranking victim of this paranoia. He was imprisoned for supposedly plotting to overthrow Stalin and in

ISBN: 9780170352581

October he was shot. All evidence of his existence as a friend of Stalin and loyal member of the Party was erased. Although the other two long-time and close colleagues of Stalin, Sergei Kirov and Nikolai Shvernik, also fell out of favour, they survived — but not in the official Soviet photographic record.

The image (above) on the far left shows General Ulysses S. Grant, commander of the Union (northern) troops during the American Civil War, 1861–65. He is, apparently, in front of his troops at City Point, Virginia. In fact, this image is a composite *[combination]* of three separate photos. The head is his own, taken from an earlier portrait photograph (see the last photo). The horse and body, however, are those of Major General Alexander M. McCook, while the background is of Confederate *[southern]* prisoners captured at the battle of Fisher's Hill, Virginia (middle photos).

In 1942, during World War Two, Italian dictator Benito Mussolini had this photograph taken (above). In order to present a more heroic picture of himself, he had the horse handler removed from the original shot.

ISBN: 9780170352581

Engagement with visual sources

Another useful way to engage with a visual source is to imagine what was happening before and after the photograph was taken, and also what was happening outside the frame of the photograph that we see.

12 ACTIVITY

Choose TWO of the photographs from pages 48–55 and use your imagination to come up with responses to each of the questions below. **Try to keep your responses realistic**.

Image number ______________

1 What might have been happening *before* the photo was taken?

- One hour before? ______________
- One day before? ______________
- One week before? ______________

2 What might have happened *after* the photo was taken?

- One hour after? ______________
- One day after? ______________
- One week after? ______________

3 What might be happening *outside* the frame of the photograph as it was being taken?

- A short distance away? ______________

 ISBN: 9780170352581

- Much further away? ______

Image number ______

1 What might have been happening *before* the photo was taken?
   - One hour before? ______
   - One day before? ______
   - One week before? ______

2 What might have happened *after* the photo was taken?
   - One hour after? ______
   - One day after? ______
   - One week after? ______

3 What might be happening *outside* the frame of the photograph as it was being taken?
   - A short distance away? ______
   - Much further away? ______

ISBN: 9780170352581

Analysing political cartoons

Usually, political cartoons are created within a context. In other words, they are commenting on events that are newsworthy at the time. For this reason, it is important to understand the context to really make sense of them. While it is much more difficult to analyse cartoons when you don't know this, the same 5W, 1H questions can provide a way into an unfamiliar cartoon. The questions all relate to what we can see in the cartoon itself.

1 **When/where** is it set? During what events/issues?
2 **Who** is featured most prominently in the cartoon? Who are the other less prominent characters?
3 **Why** do you think the cartoonist has chosen to portray the 'characters' the way he or she has?
4 **How** has the cartoonist used dialogue/captions, colour, shading, drawing style, symbols and/or caricature *[exaggerated features]* to communicate their views on the issue? (What are those views?)

And finally ...

5 **What** is the cartoonist trying to say?

1 *When/where* is the cartoon set? During what events/issues?

Without knowing the context of the cartoon, this is difficult. However, in an exam situation a cartoon (if used) will be part of a wider group of resources, so you should be able to determine the context from them. Otherwise, you might at least be able to tell if the context is, for example, a protest, in a household, a war zone, and so on. If even this is difficult, perhaps you can at least tell if the event/issue is peaceful/conflict, urban/rural, isolated/crowded, day/night ... All of these might be useful in helping decode the meaning of the cartoon. Some cartoons will have a caption or labels that will provide additional information.

2 *Who* is featured in the cartoon?

Sometimes the cartoonist will 'play it straight' and the characters will be easily recognisable — a current Prime Minister, a well-known figure from the past (such as Hitler), or a well-recognised symbol (such as a crown to represent a king or queen). More important characters will often be the largest or will be in the forefront of the cartoon.

3 *Why* do you think the cartoonist has chosen to portray the 'characters' the way he or she has?

This follows on from the 'Who?' question above. The cartoonist will have a reason for portraying his or her characters the way he or she has. You can get a sense of the power relationship between characters, or what the characters think of each other, by the way they are drawn. Common symbols used in cartoons can also help decode the meaning (see the tables on pages 62–63).

Cartoon analysis: the short version

1 Identify the context — where/when is it set?
2 Identify the main characters and the relationship between them.
3 Note carefully any written text (caption, dialogue, labels).
4 Note the use of caricature *[exaggeration of certain features]*.
5 Note the use of symbols and colour or shading.

4 *How* has the cartoonist used dialogue/captions, colour, shading, drawing style, symbols and/or caricature to communicate their views?

Many historical cartoons will only be in black and white (monochromatic), but even so the cartoonist can communicate a lot with the thickness of lines and/or shading. For example, thick, bold lines could represent powerfulness and/or danger. Heavy shading works similarly, as do 'dark' colours. Many cartoons will include dialogue between the characters and this will help with interpreting the relationship between them, and the cartoon as a whole. Any dialogue or caption might also help with this. In terms

ISBN: 9780170352581

of the characters, look also for any exaggerated features (caricature), such as an over-large smile or large claw-like hands. Whatever techniques are used, the cartoonist will be expressing his or her attitude towards the characters/issue through the way they are portrayed.

5 ***What*** **is it that the cartoonist is trying to say?**
Finally, consider all of the analysis you have done and set out your response.

13 ACTIVITY

1 From the list below, choose the appropriate 'Idea' to go with the 'Image'. Write it in the 'Idea' column. Note that the table continues over to page 62.

> Good idea, Overcoming difficulties or obstacles, Oppression, Struggle, War, Trouble, Victory, Freedom

2 In the 'Your image' column, create your own representation of the 'Idea'.

Idea	Image	Your image
	1	
	2	
	3	
	4	
	5	

Table continued over page

Idea	Image	Your image
	6	
	7	
	8	

Some common symbols used in political cartoons

The list below gives an indication of common symbols used in political cartoons. These are not the only possible ones, but they are a good start.

War and peace

Symbol	Meaning
	Dove Peace
	Olive branch Peace/forgiveness
	Vulture Preying on others/death
	Skull and crossbones/ Grim Reaper Death

Symbol	Meaning
	Laurel wreath Victory
	Sword War/death and destruction
	Phoenix Something new and powerful arising from destruction

ISBN: 9780170352581

Countries (government or people)

Uncle Sam/eagle	America
British bulldog/'John Bull'	Britain
Cockerel (rooster)	France
Bear	Russia

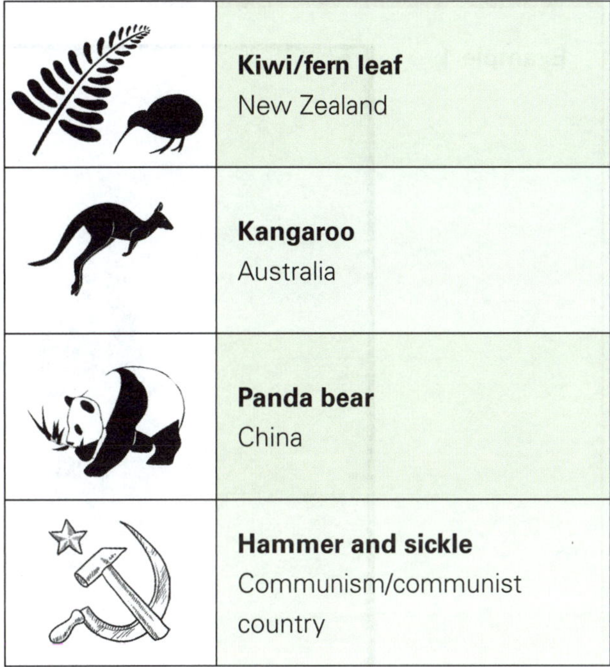

Kiwi/fern leaf	New Zealand
Kangaroo	Australia
Panda bear	China
Hammer and sickle	Communism/communist country

Virtues and vices

Tortoise	Someone who acts slowly and steadily *and ultimately wins*
Hare/rabbit	Someone who acts quickly and rushes *and ultimately loses*
Scales/a balance	Justice/fairness
Chains	Slavery
Broken chains	Freedom
Acorn	Growth/youth

Dawn	Beginning/hope
Key	Liberation/knowledge/answer to a mystery
Oak tree	Strength
Pen	Learning/knowledge
Cupid/love heart	Love
Fat man in a top hat	Capitalist/banker

ISBN: 9780170352581

ACTIVITY EXAMPLE

Example 1

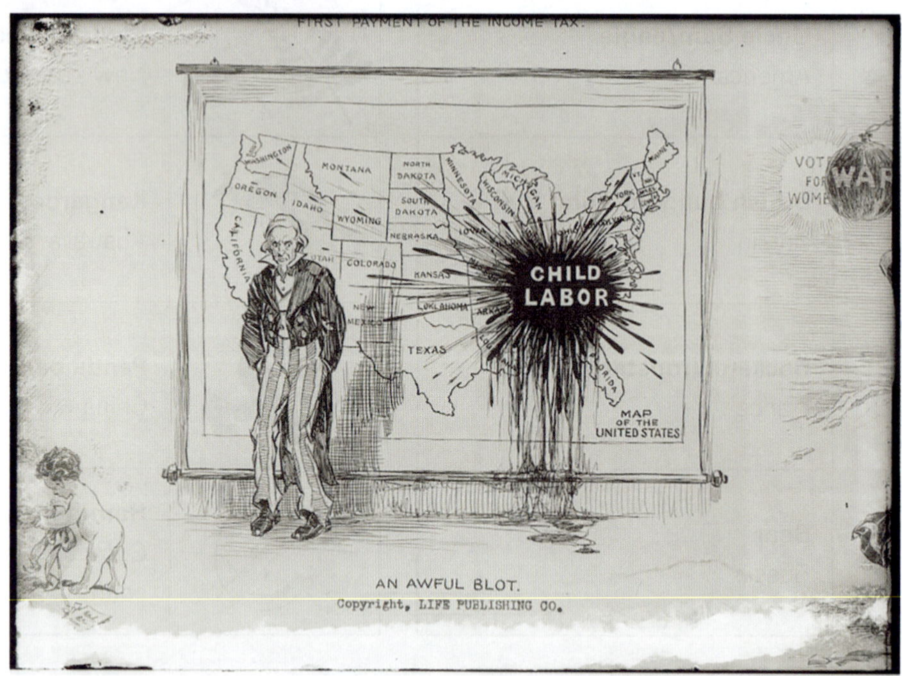

Publication date: 1914

Note: Child labour is when very young children are put to work.

1 **When/where** is it set? During what events/issues? In America, judging by the map, possibly in a classroom? The image does look 'old' and the date confirms this (1914). The map has a big ink blot on it with the words 'Child Labor'. This is backed up by the caption 'An Awful Blot'. Maybe this is set sometime when child labour was common but some people at least didn't like it. There are also some things shown hanging on the right-hand side of the frame — one says 'War' and the other looks like it says 'Votes for Women'. Hard to know what these are … political issues of the time?

2 **Who** is featured most prominently in the cartoon? Who are the other less prominent characters? The main figure looks like 'Uncle Sam' (representing America) and there's a small child who is playing with something? Given the label on the 'ink blot', perhaps the child represents child labour …?

3 **Why** do you think the cartoonist has chosen to portray the 'characters' the way he or she has? Uncle Sam seems a bit slouched … Hard to know if he's shown worried or not worried, or maybe uncomfortable. He does seem to be looking at the child. The child doesn't seem to be too concerned about anything. There doesn't appear to be any use of caricature *[exaggerated features]*.

4 **How** has the cartoonist used dialogue/captions, colour, shading, drawing style, symbols and/or caricature *[exaggerated features]* to communicate his or her views? The 'CHILD LABOR' ink blot is probably the most dramatic feature; it's quite big and looks like it's been thrown at the map quite violently ... If so, that — and the darkness of the blotch — would suggest that it's a bad thing, which would be the cartoonist's view on this issue.

And finally …

5 **What** is the cartoonist trying to say? Right, here goes! I think this is showing America in 1914 at a time, according to the cartoonist, when child labour is common and is an issue that at least some people think is terrible. The cartoonist may be trying to raise awareness or shame Americans and/or the government into taking action — this could be along with the other issues ('War' and 'Votes for Women') that maybe aren't as important to this cartoonist.

ISBN: 9780170352581

Example 2

1 **When/where** is it set? During what events/issues? It looks like it would be during World War One (1916) in an Army Medical Examiner's office. There's an Army recruitment poster on the wall.

2 **Who** is featured most prominently in the cartoon? Who are the other less prominent characters? The 'headless' soldier is most prominent, with the Army Medical Examiner there as well.

3 **Why** do you think the cartoonist has chosen to portray the 'characters' the way he or she has? Well, it seems that the huge man would be very strong and powerful. The Medical Examiner seems happy with this, and the fact that he has no head. From the Army's point of view, this cartoonist seems to be saying that this is a good combination.

Publication date: 1 July 1916

4 **How** has the cartoonist used dialogue/captions, colour, shading, drawing style, symbols and/or caricature *[exaggerated features]* to communicate his or her views? The headless man is huge and looks as though he would be very strong but at the same time unable to think for himself. The shading emphasises his muscles and makes them look more powerful. Possibly the darkness of the shading suggests a negative attitude from the cartoonist. The caption suggests that the Medical Examiner has indeed found his 'perfect soldier'.

And finally …

5 **What** is the cartoonist trying to say? During WWI the army is recruiting soldiers and the main thing is that they be strong and — equally as good — 'headless', meaning that they won't think for themselves. In this case, the cartoonist is negative towards the Army and perhaps even towards the whole war. He or she might be trying to persuade people not to sign up.

Your turn!

Note: You may find it hard to respond to all of the first four questions. Do your best, but be sure to attempt question **5** for each cartoon.

14 ACTIVITY

Cartoon A

Published 2013.

1 **When/where** is it set? During what events/issues?

2 **Who** is featured most prominently in the cartoon? Who are the other less prominent characters?

3 **Why** do you think the cartoonist has chosen to portray the 'characters' the way he or she has?

4 **How** has the cartoonist used diagloue/captions, colour, shading, drawing style, symbols and/or caricature *[exaggerated features]* to communicate his or her views on the issue?

And finally …

5 **What** is the cartoonist trying to say?

ISBN: 9780170352581

Cartoon B

Published 1985.

1 **When/where** is it set? During what events/issues?

2 **Who** is featured most prominently in the cartoon? Who are the other less prominent characters?

3 **Why** do you think the cartoonist has chosen to portray the 'characters' the way he or she has?

4 **How** has the cartoonist used diagloue/captions, colour, shading, drawing style, symbols and/or caricature *[exaggerated features]* to communicate his or her views on the issue?

And finally …

5 **What** is the cartoonist trying to say?

ISBN: 9780170352581

Cartoon C

Published 1984.

1 **When/where** is it set? During what events/issues?

2 **Who** is featured most prominently in the cartoon? Who are the other less prominent characters?

3 **Why** do you think the cartoonist has chosen to portray the 'characters' the way he or she has?

4 **How** has the cartoonist used diagloue/captions, colour, shading, drawing style, symbols and/or caricature *[exaggerated features]* to communicate his or her views on the issue?

And finally …

5 **What** is the cartoonist trying to say?

ISBN: 9780170352581

Cartoon D

Note: *The person on the left is Russian leader Nikita Khrushchev and on the right is US President John F. Kennedy. Published 1962.*

1 **When/where** is it set? During what events/issues?

2 **Who** is featured most prominently in the cartoon? Who are the other less prominent characters?

3 **Why** do you think the cartoonist has chosen to portray the 'characters' the way he or she has?

4 **How** has the cartoonist used diagloue/captions, colour, shading, drawing style, symbols and/or caricature *[exaggerated features]* to communicate his or her views on the issue?

And finally …

5 **What** is the cartoonist trying to say?

ISBN: 9780170352581

Cartoon E

Published 2013.

1 **When/where** is it set? During what events/issues?

2 **Who** is featured most prominently in the cartoon? Who are the other less prominent characters?

3 **Why** do you think the cartoonist has chosen to portray the 'characters' the way he or she has?

4 **How** has the cartoonist used diagloue/captions, colour, shading, drawing style, symbols and/or caricature *[exaggerated features]* to communicate his or her views on the issue?

And finally …

5 **What** is the cartoonist trying to say?

ISBN: 9780170352581

Cartoon F

An 'exit strategy' is a plan for a way to get out of a situation before entering it. Published 2014.

1 **When/where** is it set? During what events/issues?

2 **Who** is featured most prominently in the cartoon? Who are the other less prominent characters?

3 **Why** do you think the cartoonist has chosen to portray the 'characters' the way he or she has?

4 **How** has the cartoonist used diagloue/captions, colour, shading, drawing style, symbols and/or caricature *[exaggerated features]* to communicate his or her views on the issue?

And finally ...

5 **What** is the cartoonist trying to say?

ISBN: 9780170352581

Source reliability: fact versus opinion

History is one of the social sciences, where the 'science' part refers to the method of using evidence ('hard' facts) to arrive at conclusions, in our case about the past. The scientific method in history also involves applying critical thinking skills to the sources used; this is covered in the chapters on source reliability and primary and secondary source analysis in this workbook.

One of the key 'critical thinking' skills is to be able to determine what is fact and what is just someone's opinion, no matter how firmly or fervently *[passionately]* held. We can turn to the *Oxford English Dictionary* for a definition of the two terms:

'Critical thinking' in history means to always approach sources (both primary and secondary) with a series of questions that try to look past what is immediately obvious (see pages 33–35). It is really a mindset that treats all sources with a degree of scepticism *[suspicion]*.

FACT: information used as evidence; a thing that is known or proved to be true; the truth about events.

OPINION: a view or judgement formed about something, not necessarily based on fact or knowledge; the beliefs or views of a group or majority of people.

LYING: this is the deliberate distortion or mis-statement of the facts. It is different to having an opinion on something.

Detecting opinions

The easiest way to detect an opinion in a source is when the writer says *'I think that ...'*. Most of the time, however, opinions won't be so conveniently signalled. Basically, though, if an historian can add in the words *'I think that ...'* in front of a statement in a source, then it is likely to be an opinion.

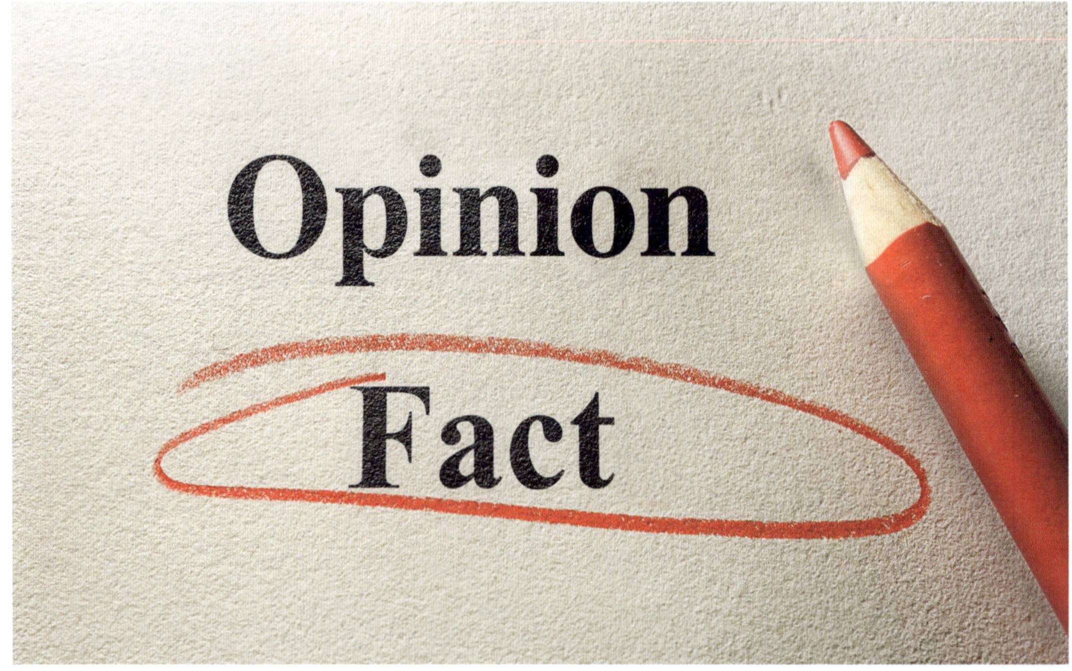

ISBN: 9780170352581

15 ACTIVITY

The following statements were published at various times in different newspapers that an historian is using for research. Identify which of these you think are FACTS and which are OPINIONS or a mixture of both.

1 All politicians are liars. ______________________

2 Wellington is a windy city. ______________________

3 Most people do not want the death penalty here in New Zealand. ______________________

4 Many people have been affected by rising petrol prices. ______________________

5 Nearly 40% of all smokers will suffer a severe smoking-related illness. ______________________

6 The protester at an anti-government rally said angrily that 'all politicians are liars'.

____

7 The guilty verdict was delivered by the jury in less than one hour, to the relief of the onlookers.

____

8 The onlookers said that they were relieved that the jury had not had any problems coming up with a guilty verdict. ______________________

9 The judge was grumpy when she heard the guilty verdict. ______________________

10 The defence lawyer said that the judge was grumpy when she heard the verdict.

____

FINISHED?

Write SIX statements that are either FACT or OPINION. Share them with someone else and get them to correctly identify what each is.

1 ______________________

____

____

2 ______________________

____

____

3 ______________________

____

____

ISBN: 9780170352581

4

5

6

When FACT and OPINION are harder to detect

To decide whether or not an *'I think that …'* could be put in front of a statement in a source, there are key types of words to look for. These are usually those that add in descriptive elements to the events being described, and thus often bring in a person's own beliefs and biases.

Example

Here is an example of a statement that is essentially neutral and thus factual:

'The man ran down the road, followed by the police officer.'

From this statement alone, what do you think might have led to the scene described?

There could, in fact, be several reasons for the situation described, such as:

- they could both be running to the scene of an accident
- they could both be running from some sort of threat (e.g. a fire or explosion)
- the man might be a peaceful protester running away from an aggressive policeman
- the man might have committed a crime.

In this case, depending on what the person reporting on this situation had seen, and even their attitude towards the police, we might get their own personal viewpoint added in. While the person making the statement might well believe it to be FACT, it would actually be OPINION.

ISBN: 9780170352581

16 ACTIVITY

Using the 'running man' situation, identify where in each of these statements there is FACT and/or OPINION (there might be a combination of both…). *NOTE: if you're not sure, put a question mark (?) so that you can discuss it with the class later.*

1 The man ran down the road, followed by the unfit police officer.

2 The man ran down the road, pursued by the uniformed police officer.

3 The man sneaked down the road, pursued by the determined police officer.

4 The guilty-looking man ran down the road, with a police officer behind him.

5 The man and the police officer ran down the road.

6 The frightened man ran down the road, followed by the shoe-less police officer.

7 The well-dressed man tore down the road, followed close behind by the sweating police officer.

8 The young man sprinted down the road, with an angry police officer puffing behind him.

ISBN: 9780170352581

6 Secondary source analysis

Usefulness

It is probably obvious that a secondary source will be useful if it helps to answer the questions we have about a certain topic. However, we can think more deeply than this about the usefulness of the secondary sources we use, especially for an inquiry. It is worth commenting on this when you do your analysis for each source.

A secondary source may be useful for an inquiry for one or more of these reasons.

One possible limitation of a secondary source that can affect its reliability is its age. If it was written and published perhaps decades ago it could be that new research or the discovery of new sources mean that it is out-of-date. Note that this isn't automatically true, but it is something to keep in mind.

- It gives a good **overview** of the whole focus question, even if it does not go into great depth. This sort of source is useful for getting a 'big picture' understanding of a topic without too much confusing detail.
- It gives **detailed coverage** of all, or just part, of the focus question. Once we have the 'big picture' understanding our inquiry may require us to go into more depth and detail.
- It contains a lot of **specific factual evidence/'hard' facts**, such as dates, names (of people, places and/or events), statistics/figures, quotes from people involved in the events/issues. All good history is based on plenty of relevant factual evidence, so a source that has this is usually good.
- It gives a **different point of view** than those found in other sources. This can include the different viewpoints of people involved in the historical events and/or historians who write about these events later.

Example of source usefulness analysis

Focus question: 'What political involvement did Maori leaders in the early 20th century have as they tried to make gains for the Maori people?'

- NOTE: the 'hard' facts here have been highlighted.

Inside the Pakeha system: the Young Maori Party

Some important Maori leaders of the early 20th century served inside the New Zealand political system. The most well known are James Carroll (Timi Kara), Apirana Ngata, Maui Pomare and Peter Buck (Te Rangi Hiroa). Each was elected to one of the four Maori seats (Northern, Western, Eastern and Southern). These leaders were nicknamed the 'Young Maori Party' (YMP), although they actually represented different political parties.

James Carroll.

Apirana Ngata.

ISBN: 9780170352581

For example, Apirana Ngata belonged to the Liberal Party and Maui Pomare to the Reform Party. Despite this, they worked together to make gains for Maori. However, to be accepted inside the Pakeha Parliament they had to excel at 'being Pakeha'. Apirana Ngata, for example, was the first Maori to gain a university degree (1897) and by the time he entered Parliament in 1905 he had three degrees — more than any other Member of Parliament, Maori or Pakeha. This was still not enough to make any significant difference, for they had only four votes between them in a 76-seat Parliament. Furthermore, those who entered Parliament were not usually traditional Maori leaders. Because of this, they struggled to earn the respect of even their own tribes. Achieving respect outside their own tribal area was even more difficult, for tribal rivalries and jealousies remained strong. Thus, many Maori saw the YMP as merely the contact point between the Maori and Pakeha worlds.
(Adapted from *Big World, Small Country*)

Maui Pomare.

Peter Buck.

Source usefulness analysis
This is useful as an **overview** of the background of the four members of the 'Young Maori Party' who became involved in New Zealand politics. It gives their tribal areas and the actual political parties they were involved in. It also contains a good range of **'hard' facts**.

Example of a source with more detailed coverage, in this case just of the work of Apirana Ngata

Focus question: 'What political involvement did Maori leaders in the early 20th century have as they tried to make gains for the Maori people?'

In 1905 Apirana Ngata ran for the Eastern Maori parliamentary seat against the long-standing Member, Wi Pere. With solid support from Ngati Porou, Ngata won by over 750 votes. He was to retain *[keep winning]* the seat, surviving challenge after challenge, until 1943. He took his duties very seriously and shunned *[avoided]* much of the social side of parliamentary life. He was a diligent *[hard-working]* member of the Native Affairs Committee and soon became James Carroll's right-hand man. He served with the Chief Justice, Sir Robert Stout, on the 1907–8 Native Land Commission. They recommended that tribes with very little remaining land should have it permanently reserved. However, tribes with plenty of land, for instance in the central North Island, could be encouraged to sell or lease some of it. Finally, they criticised governments of the past for having done nothing to encourage or assist Maori to farm their own land.

Ngata also assisted John Salmond in drafting *[writing]* the Native Land Act 1909, a massive measure to help Maori better manage their remaining lands.

Native Lands Committee 1905

ISBN: 9780170352581

Although the opposition Reform Party was the government from 1912 until 1928, Ngata had a great deal of influence, especially after Gordon Coates became Native Minister in 1921 and then Prime Minister in 1925. He and Coates had a very high regard for each other, and Ngata was often able to introduce important measures with Coates' help. An example was the establishment of the Board of Maori Ethnological Research in 1923 and the Maori Purposes Fund Control Board in 1924 to administer funds from unclaimed Maori rentals and other sources.

Yet, for all his activities Ngata remained most interested in the land reform movement. At home he arranged for Ngati Porou land holdings in the Waiapu valley to be divided up so that his people could move into dairy farming. The holdings made impressive progress, thanks to the introduction of graded cows, new milking machines, and the establishment of a co-operative dairy factory at Ruatoria. As ever, Ngata had larger aims in mind: to encourage other Maori communities to follow Ngati Porou's lead and to persuade the government to support Maori land development. His first success with other tribes came in 1922 when he persuaded Tuhoe to follow Ngati Porou's example. Others soon followed suit as younger educated Maori came onboard and took up the work.

(Adapted from *Te Ara*)

Source usefulness

This source does not talk much about other leaders but it gives good detail on how Apirana Ngata, one of the key Maori leaders of the early 20th century, became involved in politics. It explains how he rose to high positions and talks especially about his work on Maori land. It also contains plenty of 'hard' facts (highlighted). The image also shows that Ngata is involved in politics (Native Lands Committee).

Selecting relevant information/annotations

During an inquiry, once you have found a relevant source — whether it be primary or secondary, 'hard copy' or electronic — you'll need to indicate in some way the 'best bits' that *directly answer your focus question(s).* The easiest way is probably to use a highlighter. Once you've done that you'll then want to annotate/write margin notes against the highlighted sections. The purpose of the annotations is to show your understanding of the highlighted pieces by briefly explaining how they help to answer the focus question. This is not the same as simply summarising what's there (after all, both you and your teacher who is marking your work can read it!) but going a step further to note *how* it helps.

Keep in mind that we must find the information that answers the focus question in the source itself; it must directly provide the evidence. Sometimes it is easy to fall into the trap of highlighting something that does not *directly* answer the focus question but, with some explaining by you, *might* well answer it ... This is not acceptable 'evidence from the source' if you have to 'fill in the gaps'. See Example 2 below.

Example 1

Note below how only the most relevant pieces have been highlighted. The annotations/margin notes start by briefly summarising the highlighted information and then the final sentence makes the link to the focus question clear.

ISBN: 9780170352581

Focus question: **'Why did Hitler invade the Soviet Union in 1941?'**

The invasion of the Soviet Union by Hitler was the result of his concern that Germany did not have enough farmland to produce the agricultural goods that the country needed. He knew of the raw material and land resources of America and Britain's empire and wanted the same for Germany. He was also familiar with the expansion of the American frontier in the 18th and 19th centuries that resulted in the destruction of the Native American Indians. The land and resources that this provided for the settlers was an enormous benefit to the American economy. It is hard to imagine that America would be the same economic giant as it is today if its resource base had stayed in the possession of its rightful owners. Hitler often used America's example to call for the pushing aside of the Polish and Russian populations to the east to provide land and resources for Germany's farmers. However, Germany's agricultural weakness is evidenced by its low land-labour ratio (that is, workers per hectare of land), but Poland and the Ukraine had even less land per person. Thus simply acquiring the land to the east could not in fact have solved Germany's economic problems; more efficiency on German farms was what was needed.

Hitler felt Germany needed more farmland. He also knew that in the past America had taken its land from the Indians, and it had been good for their economy. So it seems that economic reasons were behind the invasion, as well as the example set by America's settlers.

Example 2

Note below how the first part is correctly highlighted and annotated, but the second part does not directly answer the focus question. It should not be highlighted!

Focus question: **'Why did Hitler invade the Soviet Union in 1941?'**

In Hitler's book *Mein Kampf* (*My Struggle*) he explains his views on many issues, particularly what he called the 'twin evils' of the Jewish race and communism. He openly states that the future of Germany 'has to lie in the acquisition *[gaining]* of land in the East, at the expense of Russia.' This was in line with his policy of Lebensraum — extra 'living space' for the German people. Such open views of hostility towards Russia made it so much more of a shock when the German-Soviet Non-aggression Pact was revealed in 1939. This pact promised ten years of peace between the two countries. Only Russia's leader Stalin took the pact seriously. In June of 1941, just two years after signing it, Hitler acted on the task that he had in mind all along: an invasion of Russia.

Hitler had for a long time wanted more land in the east, *so a reason for the invasion was to expand German territory.*

This pact would have given Hitler extra time to build up his armies so that he could invade.

This is in fact true, *but it does not actually say it in the text!* The text is like evidence in a court and you can't 'add in' something that isn't there — you might be wrong! This part should not really have been highlighted.

ISBN: 9780170352581

1 ACTIVITY

For each piece of text below:

- highlight the correct part(s) that directly answer the focus question
- write in brief annotations that show the link to the focus question.

1 **Focus question**: **'How did the government respond to the different forms of Maori leadership?'**

Faced with a Pakeha government that neglected their concerns, Maori leaders had three main choices. Some became part of the Pakeha system. They did this by being elected to Parliament in one of the four Maori seats. From there they worked inside the Pakeha government to try to change things. However, with only four Maori members they did not have much influence over the government. A second option, taken up eventually by some traditional tribal leaders, was to work alongside the Pakeha system. At first, governments paid little attention to these tribal leaders. Soon, however, officials came to realise that they provided an effective link to Maori communities. A third option, taken up by one notable Maori leader in the 20th century, was to build a separate community, outside direct Pakeha influence. The government did not like separatist movements and, as with earlier cases, responded with armed force.

2 **Focus question**: **'What social changes occurred in the 1920s in many countries?'**

In the 1920s, there was a reaction amongst the public to the gloom of World War One and the hardship it represented. This period, lasting until the Great Depression began in 1929, has become known as the 'Jazz Age' or the 'Roaring Twenties'. Jazz music came from African-American origins, but was adapted to be acceptable to a white American audience. The newly developed commercial radio stations helped spread it, and its popularity grew. With it came new dance crazes such as the Charleston. Young people in the 1920s were very much influenced by jazz, and it became the 'sound track' of a rebellion against the traditional culture of previous generations.

From America, the music and its associated culture spread across the Atlantic to Europe (and, eventually, to New Zealand too). In America, those who embraced the new ways were known as 'flappers', and in Britain as 'Bright Young People'. Well-to-do women adopted daring new fashions such

ISBN: 9780170352581

as short skirts, make-up and bobbed haircuts. They took up drinking and smoking in public, began wearing make-up, and went out unchaperoned *[without an older woman as escort]*. The money flowing due to the Dawes Plan helped create a wider sense of prosperity. The bad times, it seemed, were over.

3 Focus question: **'How did governments in different countries deal with the problems of the Great Depression, 1929–35?'**

Sweden was one of the few countries where the people survived the Depression relatively unscathed *[unharmed]*. Sweden already had a history of providing social welfare for its people, dating back to 1914. By 1925, all schoolchildren were being provided with a free daily meal. In 1931, the Social Democratic Party won the election in a landslide *[sweeping]* victory. The new government provided unemployment benefits, family allowances and old-age pensions, as well as supporting sickness funds. Sweden rejected the view held in the US and other countries such as New Zealand at this time, that poverty was the fault of the individual. In these countries, government support for the people was minimal. However, when the first Labour government was elected in New Zealand in 1935, it followed policies similar to Sweden's.

In Japan, the military became more influential due to the Depression. Japan had industrialised *[built factories]* rapidly after WWI, and was badly affected in the early 1930s when other countries cut back their imports of Japanese products. Nearly 50 percent of Japan's heavy industry closed, and the vital silk export trade was destroyed. However, Japan's main problem was different to that of most countries. Japan lacked the raw materials it needed for its factories, and these had to be bought from overseas.

During the 1920s, Japan had imported iron, rubber and oil to maintain its strong economic growth. Most of these resources came from the United States. In the 1930s, Japan lacked the money to buy them. Elements within the Japanese government, and nationalists *[strongly patriotic people]* outside it, felt that an alternative would be to simply take over resource-rich territories.

ISBN: 9780170352581

4 Focus question: **'What actions were taken by the government in an attempt to maintain the British nature of "New Zealand identity"?'**

As the war clouds again gathered in Europe in the late 1930s, most Pakeha New Zealanders still felt that they were British. Many Maori also felt part of the British Empire, to greater or lesser degrees. The experiences of WWI made many New Zealanders feel not so much that they had developed a separate identity, but that they had proved themselves to be 'better British'. Smaller groups, such as the relatively few Chinese, Indians, Lebanese and Dalmatians in the country, did their best to be part of this identity. If not, they at least tried to be inconspicuous *[low key]* in terms of their own cultural values.

One of the 'threats' to New Zealand's sense of 'better British' identity came from American cultural influences. From the early 1920s, concern was being raised about the American presence in the media. In 1927, 350 out of the 400 films shown in New Zealand were from the United States. This led to the introduction of a law in 1928 for quotas of British films. By the 1930s, the proportion of British films being shown had increased to 50 percent.

When American radio serials began to be broadcast in the early 1930s, there was further criticism of them as 'un-British'. One critic noted that New Zealanders were imitating Americans by saying 'Okay, baby'. Apart from a brief period during WWII, American radio serials were banned until the 1960s. Australian radio serials were deemed *[considered]* to be more acceptable, and they became popular.

5 Focus question: **'What strategies did Keith Park use to protect England from attack?'**

Keith Park was born in Thames, Coromandel. He was schooled at King's College in Auckland, as well as Otago Boys' High School in Dunedin. In WWI he fought at Gallipoli, and then at the Battle of the Somme. It was during this time that he came to appreciate the importance of aerial reconnaissance *['spying' from the air]* over enemy positions. In October 1916 he was blown off his horse by a German shell and his Army days were over. He decided to join the Royal Flying Corps. By the end of WWI, he had earned the Military Cross for shooting down a German aircraft and damaging three others. He also received the Distinguished Flying Cross and the French Croix de Guerre, among other awards. After the war he became a flight instructor.

ISBN: 9780170352581

He steadily rose through the ranks to become a staff officer to Air Chief Marshal Hugh Dowding by 1938.

In April 1940, prior to the fall of France and the Battle of Britain, Air Vice Marshal Park was put in charge of defending the skies above London and southeast England. In this role, he organised fighter patrols over the French coast. He also co-ordinated fighter defences against German attacks during the Battle of Britain. He supported Dowding's plan to only deploy *[put into action]* a small number of fighters to resist each wave of the *Luftwaffe*. This was because the Royal Air Force simply did not have enough planes or pilots. To preserve this limited strength, Park ordered the pilots to focus on shooting down just the German bombers. It was these, and not the escorting fighters, that would cause the most damage. To inspire his men, as often as possible he flew his personal Hurricane fighter — the 'OK1' — to visit the airfields where the pilots were stationed.

After the war, Air Chief Marshal Sir Arthur Tedder (who was also Deputy Supreme Commander under General Dwight Eisenhower for the 'D-Day' invasion) noted that: *'If any one man won the Battle of Britain, [park] did. I do not believe it is realised how much that one man, with his leadership, his calm judgement and his skill, did to save, not only this country [Britain], but the world.'*

6 Focus question: **'What impact did New Zealand women gaining the vote in 1893 have on government policies?'**

From the late 19th century, the state *[government]* was influential in determining women's roles. One way was through the promotion of high birth rates for Pakeha. By 1900, the average birth rate had dropped to 3.5 children per family, from seven in 1876. There was great concern that Pakeha were committing 'race suicide' by not breeding enough. Women were thus encouraged to be mothers. However, this policy was ineffective, and birth rates continued to fall. It would take the trauma of World War Two before they rose dramatically. Soldiers returning from the conflict were looking for the stability and normality that a family could provide.

Wage laws were another means by which women were 'guided' out of the workforce and into the home. Restrictions were placed on the hours and type of work that women could do. For example, they could not do heavy lifting or night

ISBN: 9780170352581

shifts. (At night, women were meant to be tending to the needs of husband and children.) While most women were indeed mothers, up to the 1930s about 18 percent of women were in the workforce. A significant number worked as domestic *[household]* servants, or in factories or office jobs. A few were professionals, such as librarians, teachers and nurses. In all cases, they were paid less than men. A man's role as head of the family and main income earner was put into law in 1936. The minimum wage for male workers was set at a level where a man could provide for a wife and three children. This was called the 'family wage' and remained in place until the 1960s. The welfare benefits introduced by the Labour government in the 1930s were also based on the man of the house being able to provide for his.

A final area of state intervention to shape the role of women was in education. Girls in the first half of the 20th century were supposed to learn how to be wives and mothers. Compulsory domestic education was thus introduced in 1917. In their courses, girls learned about cooking, cleaning and child-care. In reality, however, most girls preferred to do more academic courses. This was despite the warnings of people like Truby King, the founder of Plunket. He claimed that studying hard would affect the ability of girls to have healthy children.

TODAY IN HISTORY

JULY

1/7/1200	The Chinese first begin using sunglasses. Judges wore them to conceal facial expressions during trials
5/7/1946	Bikini swimsuits modelled for the first time in Paris
8/7/1844	The flagstaff at Kororareka (Russell) is cut down for the first time by Hone Heke
10/7/1985	Greenpeace anti-nuclear protest vessel the *Rainbow Warrior* is bombed by French agents
11/7/1821	Hongi Hika returns from a visit to London, having traded gifts for muskets in Port Jackson (Sydney)
16/7/622	Islamic era begins when Muhammed starts his escape from Mecca to Medina
20/7/1969	Neil Armstrong and Edwin Aldrin step onto the moon
23/7/1904	Ice cream cone is invented by Charles Menches
27/7/1586	Sir Walter Raleigh brings the first tobacco to England, as well as potatoes (from present-day Colombia)

ISBN: 9780170352581

7 Inquiry source analysis template and exemplar

Inquiry source template

The template below provides you with a framework to ensure that you think carefully about the sources that you use. The information that you gather here will be very useful in your inquiry evaluation.

Focus question: (Write it in here. Attach your evidence from a website, a book, and so on, as a separate sheet.)

1 How this evidence helps to answer the focus question

Summarise very briefly *in your own words* the main ideas in the evidence/information you have found. Use your notes from your annotations (highlighting/margin notes) to write this brief summary; this can form part of your inquiry evaluation.

2 How USEFUL this evidence is for helping to answer the focus question

Use the points below to guide your comments (see page 76 for more detail). You may simply highlight the relevant points.

- It gives a good **overview**.
- It gives **detailed coverage** of all, or just part of, the focus question.
- It contains a lot of **specific factual evidence/'hard' facts**.
- It gives a **different point-of-view** than those found in my other sources.

Source reliability: (Copy and paste a short relevant piece from the 'About Us' page of a website, or other information you've found that gives some details about the person/organisation that created the information. *Highlight the most relevant sections.*)

My comment: *Refer to the information you highlighted above* and summarise briefly *in your own words* why the source is reliable. See points A–G in the box below for guidance, as well as pages 27–28.

Some reasons why you might *trust* a source:

A It is a **primary source** (created by, or using quotes from, someone actually involved with the events at or near the time they occurred).

B The writer is **well qualified** (for example, an expert) and can speak with good knowledge about the event or person.

C The source (whether website or book or something else) is created by a **well-known and trusted organisation/publisher**.

D Other sources provide similar information/facts (provide *examples* of this).

E It has plenty of '**hard**' **facts** that can be checked.

F It has a good number of **references** and/or a **bibliography**.

G The language used by the author is reasonable, without being strongly one-sided or emotive.

Source details

- For a website: URL + date visited.
- For a book: author, title, place of publication, date of publication, page number(s).

TODAY IN HISTORY

AUGUST

13/8/1921	NZ beats South Africa 13–5 in their first rugby encounter, at Carisbrook (Dunedin)
18/8/1920	US women get the vote
29/8/1914	NZ forces occupy Western Samoa. The few German troops stationed there surrender without a shot being fired
30/8/30 BC	Cleopatra of Egypt commits suicide by letting an asp (snake) bite her
31/8/1968	West Indian batsman Garfield Sobers becomes the first cricketer to score six sixes off one over in first-class cricket, against England

ISBN: 9780170352581

Inquiry source exemplar

The piece of evidence below was found on a website. It could also have come from a book, or from notes taken while watching a video or listening to a podcast. Notice how the best bits that *clearly* answer the focus question have been highlighted.

Brief annotations (margin notes) explain the highlighted information in terms of how it helps to answer the focus question.

See the following page for the analysis, done on the template.

Focus question: '**What impact did Hitler have on different groups in Germany due to his actions/policies?**'

For ordinary people, life was good, and many Germans even today look back and remember the years before 1939 as happy years. Nazi economic policies gave full employment through work programmes such as 'Strength through Joy'. Prosperity and financial security seemed to have returned after the dark years of the Great Depression. Many observers stated that there seemed to be no poverty in Germany, while the Strength through Joy programme (KdF) gave some people fun and holidays.

Overseas reports mostly focused on the success of Hitler's government in overcoming the economic problems that had faced Germany. There were few voices raised in concern when Hitler began to overturn the terms of the hated Treaty of Versailles. Even the reoccupation of the Rhineland in 1936 brought forth no strong response. While the increasingly hostile measures taken against the Jews were viewed as unnecessarily harsh, this did not dent the overall positive view of Germany in the 1930s.

The 'Beauty of Work' movement (SdA) gave people pride in what they were doing. Law and order was improved (few people locked their doors), the autobahns (motorways) also improved transport, and frequent ceremonies, rallies, and coloured flags all added excitement.

Nazi propaganda gave people hope, while Nazi racial philosophy gave people self-belief. There was trust in Adolf Hitler and he gave a sense of security (one German woman told the American reporter Nora Wall: 'He is my mother and my father. He keeps me safe from all harm.')

There were, however, a few drawbacks. Wages fell, and strikers could be shot – the Nazis worked closely with the businessmen to make sure that the workforce were as controlled as possible. There was loss of personal freedoms; for example, freedom of speech. All culture had to be German: music had to be Beethoven or Wagner or German folk songs – or Nazi songs. All actors had to be members of the Nazi party and only books by approved authors could be read.

This shows that Nazi Germany wasn't bad for everyone. People had jobs, fun and holidays (the Strength through Joy programme). It does say 'some' people, though, so not everyone.

This brief note shows that the Jews did not have such a good time.

There was another Nazi programme 'Beauty of Work' that made life better. People felt safer and it was more exciting. Probably this was just for 'some' people, too.

People trusted Hitler as he gave them hope.

This section shows that not everything was good for even the 'some' people mentioned above. Their lives were controlled and they had to obey, even in terms of the music they listened to!

Source: http://www.johndclare.net/

Focus question: 'What impact did Hitler have on different groups in Germany due to his actions/policies?'

How this evidence helps to answer the focus question

Summarise very briefly *in your own words* the main ideas in the evidence/information you have found. Use your notes from your annotations (highlighting/margin notes) to write this brief summary; this can form part of your inquiry evaluation.

This evidence is quite broad and it doesn't go into much detail on how individual groups in Germany were affected by Hitler's policies and actions, but it does give me a good overview. It tells me that many Germans had improvements in their lives such as more jobs and excitement, people felt safer and transport was improved. Not all Germans enjoyed these changes, however (e.g. the Jews), and even the German people themselves had restrictions on their lives, such as the music they could listen to and the books they could read.

How USEFUL this evidence is for helping to answer the focus question

Use the point below to guide your comments (see page 76 for more detail). You may simply highlight the relevant points.

- It gives a good overview.
- It gives **detailed coverage** of all, or just part of, the focus question.
- It contains a lot of **specific factual evidence/'hard' facts**. *(there are some, rather than lots!)*
- It gives a **different point-of-view** than those found in my other sources.

Source reliability: (Copy and paste a short relevant piece from the 'About Us' page of a website, or other information you've found that gives some details about the person/organisation that created the information. *Highlight the most relevant sections.*)

John D Clare studied Modern history at Oxford University, graduating in 1974. He has a Post-graduate Certificate in Specific Learning Difficulties. He started his teaching career in a Special Centre for children with brain damage in an inner city teaching unit, but went as Head of History in 1979 to Greenfield School, County Durham, where he eventually became Deputy Headteacher (Raising Achievement). Described in the educational journal *Teaching History* as 'the best teacher out', he prefers the report from a previous Ofsted inspection — 'a mixture of Jesus Christ, Laurence Olivier and Genghis Khan'. He is the author of some 100 history textbooks, such as *The Slave Trade* and *Italian Renaissance*, learning packs and children's history books, which have been published in 19 countries and 17 different languages.

My comment: *Refer to the information you highlighted above* and summarise briefly *in your own words* why the source is reliable. See points A–G in the box on page 86 for guidance, as well as pages 27–28.

The author has studied history at University level and then has been a teacher for a long time, including Head of history. The journal 'Teaching History' seems to think he's very good and he's written a lot of history books. He isn't, however, a history professor and he does write children's history books, so he's not really an 'expert' but is still knowledgeable [Point B]. *His article also has hard facts* [Point E] *and the language seems to be neutral — he also points out both the good and the bad things about Hitler* [Point G].

Source details

- http://www.johndclare.net/ 16 June 2025

ISBN: 9780170352581

8 Essay structure

Structuring an essay

The main job of an essay is to communicate information clearly to the reader. An essay responds to a question or a topic statement. To do this, essays follow a certain structure:

- **Introduction** — this tells the reader **briefly** what's coming up in the main body.
- **Main body** — this contains **paragraphs** that communicate the information.
- **Conclusion** — this summarises the essay and tells the reader **briefly** what they've just read!

The backbone is like the 'argument' that runs through the essay, while the bones are like the topic sentences that help the paragraphs 'flesh out' the main body.

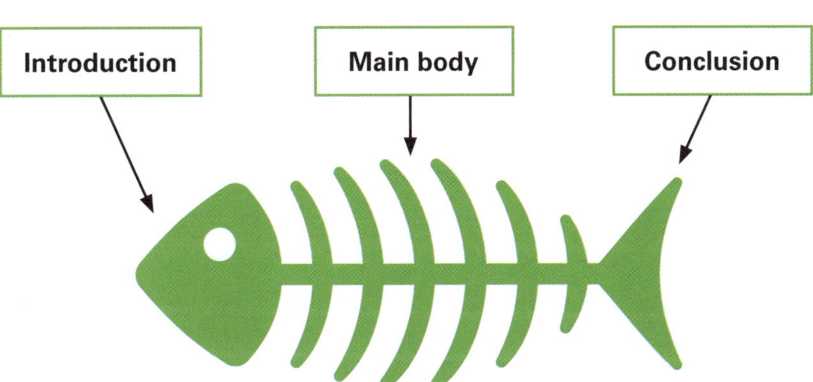

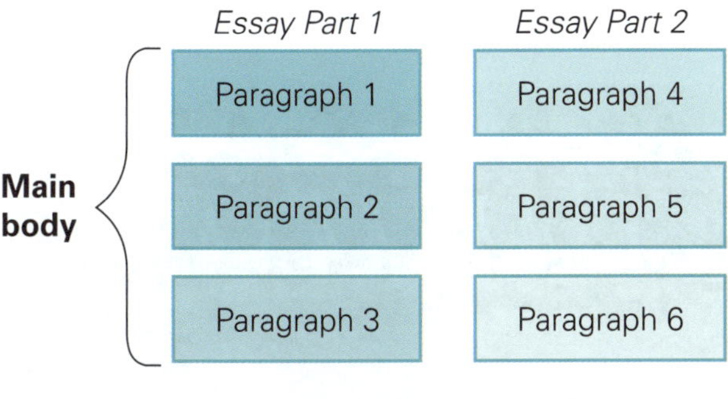

Here is another way of showing the same idea. In this case, the two-part essay (as Level 1 exam essays are) has three paragraphs for each of the two parts.

Note how the introduction deals with *both* parts of the essay question/topic, and then this is followed by the main body paragraphs. Similarly, the conclusion also deals with both parts of the essay question/topic together.

The number of paragraphs an essay has will be determined by the number of main points you wish to make as part of your answer. See the following pages for more on this.

Essay-writing skills: Why do we need to structure our ideas?

Below are the key words from two paragraphs on the early history of rugby relations between New Zealand and South Africa. While it might look interesting, it's not easy to clearly follow what the main points are.

This example shows why it is important to structure our ideas so that the reader can follow them. Remember that when you're writing an essay, *you* are the *expert*, and your main goal is to make your ideas available to the reader. You need to help the reader as much as you can, and you do this with clear structure.

Here's the same text, filled out into proper sentences in two structured paragraphs.

A GREAT RIVALRY: SOUTH AFRICA

Links with South Africa began with a Springbok tour to New Zealand in 1921. South Africans loved their rugby as much as New Zealanders did, and a great rivalry developed. The 1921 tour included a match against a Maori team, which the Springboks won 9–8. One South African journalist was appalled that the Springboks should have to play a 'coloured' Maori team. He noted that the only thing worse than this was the enthusiastic support which the Pakeha crowd gave them. This was 'too much for the Springboks who were frankly disgusted.' Because of this view, Maori players were omitted from a tour to South Africa in 1928. When the Springboks returned in 1937, the Rugby Union decided not to field a Maori team.

Even after the introduction of the apartheid laws in South Africa in 1948, the New Zealand Rugby Union did not challenge the exclusion of Maori from tours involving the Springboks. In effect, South Africa had extended apartheid to New Zealand rugby. When Maori were excluded from a tour to South Africa in 1949, public protest was voiced. Some people pointed with disgust to the similarities between the racial policy of apartheid and those of the Nazis. The President of the Returned Services Association, Sir Howard Kippenberger, expressed strong opposition on behalf of the soldiers who had died fighting Nazism. World War Two had begun to change views on racial issues.

ISBN: 9780170352581

Review of a basic literacy skill

1 ACTIVITY

Apostrophes have been left out of the following sentences — add them in.

1 At a rally in 1939, Hitler announced: 'Weve entered a new era, and the peoples self-belief will be put to the test.'

2 According to Prime Minister Lange, New Zealands anti-nuclear law proved its worth when it was most needed.

3 Its been a long time since theyve visited the battle site.

4 The womans hat nearly blew off its owners head!

5 The womens suffrage movement was finally successful in winning the vote in 1893.

6 'Well, thats about it,' she said, although they werent actually finished with their apostrophe tasks.

7 'It isnt fair; we cant be expected to do the whole classs work ourselves,' said those who had finished their activities quickly.

8 'Practice makes perfect,' the teacher said as she took the boys work in but let the girls continue, as theyd had less time.

Tips

1 An apostrophe is used for 'contractions'; that is, when a letter or letters are dropped. For example:
- is not = isn't
- cannot = can't
- it is = it's
- it has = it's

2 Apostrophes are also used to signal that someone (or something) possesses something else. For example:
- The bowl belonging to the **dog** = **The dog's bowl.**
- The bowl belonging to the **dogs** = **The dogs' bowl.**

As always in the English language, there is an exception.
- **It's** is only ever **it is** (or **it has**)
- There is *NO* **its'**.

Should've, could've, would've ...

Many students use these words incorrectly, writing them how they *think* they hear them:
- should *of*, could *of*, would *of* ... WRONG!

The correct spellings for these words are actually contractions *[shortenings]* of:
- should *have*, could *have*, would *have*.

The correct spelling of the contractions is:
- should've, could've, would've.

Note how they *sound* like the incorrect spelling.

9 Paragraph structure

Paragraphs describe and explain only *one main idea* each. These main ideas all relate to and help answer the essay question/ topic. You can use 'TEE' to help you remember the paragraph structure:

Topic sentence — tells the reader briefly what *one* main idea is going to be talked about in the paragraph, while also using *key words* from the essay question/topic to make the link to it clear.

Explanation — these sentences tell the reader about the main idea in some detail.

Examples — these back up the main point and explanation, just like a lawyer needs evidence to *prove* a point by providing *facts*. These can be:

- names (of people, places, events and organisations)
- dates of events
- statistics (numbers)
- short quotes from people such as eyewitnesses or experts.

Normally the 'Explanation' and 'Examples' are blended in together, rather than written separately.

At this level, the guidance given here is for a solid, 'by-the-rules' essay and paragraph structure. As you develop your own writing style and advance into the higher levels of history (including university), this foundation can be further developed.

There are many different mnemonics (memory assists) to help remember paragraph structures. You might also know of:

- KEE
- SEX
- TEX
- PEEL

All of these share a similar idea of structure.

Note: some paragraph structures have a fourth part, often an '**L**' for 'link back to the question/topic'. This can be a useful addition but is not vital at this level.

ISBN: 9780170352581

Planning your essay's paragraphs

A paragraph is essentially a 'bite-size' chunk of related information. Just as you wouldn't (usually) try to stuff a whole sandwich into your mouth in one go, we also don't want to 'stuff' all the information we know about a topic into our reader's head in one go. Bite-sized pieces of a sandwich are far easier to consume and digest; so too are 'bite-sized' paragraphs.

Formal writing rules are designed to help us communicate information clearly, so that the reader can follow our ideas. To help the reader, we try to group together information that is similar — into **paragraphs**. A paragraph is thus like a **kete (basket) of similar information**. We do this grouping of ideas as part of the planning phase of essay writing.

1 ACTIVITY

1 Sort the following into four *kete* or 'baskets' of similar items/information.

2 What 'label' would you put on each 'basket' of similar information to describe what is in it?

Mitsubishi	Orange	Pear	Subaru
Kumara	Labrador	Pumpkin	Apple
Spinach	Peach	Poodle	Ford
Silver beet	Toyota	German shepherd	Potato
Doberman	Holden	Lemon	Fox terrier

'Kete 1' label: ____________

'Kete 2' label: ____________

'Kete 3' label: ____________

'Kete 4' label: ____________

Burger King	Horror	Mathematics	Science fiction
Pop	McDonald's	Comedy	Hip-hop
History	Action	Rap	English
Pizza Hut	Rock	Science	Punk
KFC	Romance	Subway	Geography

'Kete 1' label: ____________

'Kete 2' label: ____________

'Kete 3' label: ____________

'Kete 4' label: ____________

These activities may seem simple, but they are still useful to illustrate how to think about planning your paragraphs. Each paragraph needs to focus on one main point (which will almost always include a number of supporting points). The 'labels' for each kete in these activities are in effect the main point for each paragraph.

ISBN: 9780170352581

'Hard' facts vs 'soft' facts

Historians always favour the use of 'hard' facts to support their understanding of the past. You should look to use 'hard' facts as often as possible, rather than the alternative 'soft' facts.

In history, 'hard' facts are always preferable, and these include:

- names (of people, places, events, organisations)
- dates of events
- statistics (numbers)
- short quotes from people such as eye-witnesses or experts.

A 'soft' fact is similar to a generalisation, or general statement. For example, it is true to say: *'During the six years of World War Two many thousands of New Zealanders died.'* However, 'many thousands' is not a 'hard' (specific) fact: here is a 'hard' fact version of this same statement. *'During the six years of World War Two 11,928 New Zealanders died.'* It would also be quite acceptable (although slightly less accurate) to say that *'... nearly 12,000 New Zealanders died.'*

Examples

'Soft' facts/generalisations	'Hard' facts
By the year 1900, only *a fraction* of New Zealand land remained in Maori ownership.	By the year 1900, only about *12% (3.2 million hectares)* of New Zealand land remained in Maori ownership.
Native Americans did not get full United States citizenship rights until *relatively recently.*	Native Americans did not get full United States citizenship rights until *the Indian Citizenship Act of 1924.*
Maori were considered New Zealand citizens under British law *quite early on.*	Maori were considered New Zealand citizens under British law *with the signing of the Treaty of Waitangi in 1840.*

TODAY IN HISTORY

SEPTEMBER

1/9/1939	Germany invades Poland, sparking what would become World War Two
4/9/1781	Los Angeles founded by Spanish settlers and named El Pueblo de Nuestra Senora La Reina de Los Angeles
6/9/1918	Mrs Elizabeth Yates, first female mayor (of Auckland) in the British Empire, dies
7/9/1776	First submarine used in warfare makes an unsuccessful attempt to attach a mine to a British flagship in New York harbour
7/9/2009	At 6 am Samoa changes from driving on the right to driving on the left.
10/9/1842	Death of New Zealand's first Governor William Hobson (buried in Grafton cemetery, Auckland)
11/9/2001	Al-Qaeda attacks with hijacked aircraft New York's Twin Towers and the Pentagon.
14/9/1868	Golf's first recorded hole-in-one at Prestwick's 166-yard eighth hole
17/9/1665	Great bubonic plague breaks out in London
25/9/1818	First transfusion of human blood at Guy's Hospital in London
26/9/1830	Baptism of six Maori adults at the Kerikeri mission, by Reverend William Yate
29/9/1829	First police patrols begin in London, nicknamed 'Bobbies' after Home Secretary Sir Robert Peel

ISBN: 9780170352581

2 ACTIVITY

1 In the following text, highlight where you think a 'soft' fact could be replaced by a better 'hard' fact.

2 Sometimes in the text there are no 'hard' or 'soft' facts where there should be! If you think that there should be some additional specific evidence, note this too.

NOTE: in some cases specific 'hard' facts might not be available to the historian; a 'soft' fact or generalisation would in this case be acceptable, as long as there was at least some sort of evidence in their research to support it.

THE 1953–1954 ROYAL TOUR TO NEW ZEALAND

One of the clearest indications of how most New Zealanders felt about Britain was the 1953–1954 Royal Tour by the Queen. This was a major event for several reasons. Firstly, Pakeha New Zealanders — and a number of Maori — still identified closely with Britain and the Commonwealth. Several years earlier New Zealanders had still been dying as part of Britain's effort to defeat the enemy in the war. Also, most of New Zealand's import and export trade was with Britain. Furthermore, many of the country's immigrants at the time were from just one country. Finally, New Zealand in the 1950s was booming. Wartime restrictions were over, and a New Zealander had conquered Mt Everest for the first time. The Royal Tour — the first by a reigning *[ruling]* monarch — seemed to cap off a perfect year.

The Queen and her husband toured through many towns and attended a large number of different functions in five weeks. In some places sheep were dyed red, white and blue in displays of patriotism. In others, instructions were given on how to plant flower gardens in similar patriotic colours. Towns tried to outdo each other in the size and spectacle of their greeting. Children formed an important part of most receptions. This was in order to reinforce in a new generation the traditional ties with Britain. It was also to show off the healthy vibrancy of the country.

All was not entirely well on the tour. The Queen had been in the country for only a short time when a rail disaster occurred, in which a large number of people died. More problems arose when the government announced that there would be only one Maori reception for the Queen. The Minister of Maori Affairs showed insensitivity to the Maori desire to demonstrate their loyalty along tribal lines: *'So far as the Queen herself is concerned, they will just be the Maori people. She will not be concerned to know from what tribes they have come.'* Initially there were no plans to attend a welcome at the base of the Maori King Movement. In the end, the government gave in and scheduled a three-minute visit. The Queen, impressed by the preparations and reception, ended up staying longer.

10 Planning

Grouping information into key ideas: Version 1

Note: if you want more of a challenge go straight to Activity 2, page 97. It is a version with THREE categories of information.

The Polynesian Panthers: background information

The Polynesian Panther Party (PPP) came into existence in mid-1971, led by the Tongan Will 'Ilolahia. 'Ilolahia was a former gang member who came to the realisation that his gang lifestyle had no future. Instead, he turned to education and political awareness as a means to help not just himself, but also other young Pasifika people who were heading into trouble. This worked, and the PPP attracted a number of young people, most of them aged around 18. They were from Tongan, Samoan and Cook Island backgrounds, as well as Maori.

Below is some information that you have found during an inquiry about the Polynesian Panthers. You realise that there is a bit too much to cram into one paragraph, so you think about how to sensibly divide it into TWO separate categories.

1 ACTIVITY

1 Read through the information (**a** – **i**) on the next page and **highlight/identify any common words/ideas/types of actions that could be grouped together**. Write the letters of each piece of information (**a** – **i**) into one of the 'Information Group' boxes below, according to how you think it should be grouped.

2 What 'label' would you put on each kete/group of ideas?

Label 1:	**Label 2:**
Information Group 1:	**Information Group 2:**

ISBN: 9780170352581

- **a** In late 1971, the Panthers carried out their first protest action, against a tour to South Africa by a men's softball team.
- **b** In 1972, the Panthers participated in anti-Vietnam War protest marches.
- **c** A Tenants' Aid Brigade was set up later in 1972 to help Pasifika people threatened with eviction *[removal]* from their rental properties.
- **d** In 1974, several Panther members travelled to Wellington to present submissions *[viewpoints]* on racism to the government.
- **e** The Panthers supported the Maori Land March protest *[hikoi]* in 1975.
- **f** The Panthers were successful in getting traffic lights installed at a busy Ponsonby intersection, where children were getting badly hurt.
- **g** Tigi Ness was expelled from Mt Albert Grammar School in the early 1970s for refusing to cut his Afro: 'A lot of students from university heard I was being expelled, and the Polynesian Panthers had just been formed, so as I was leaving school they came up with placards and protested: "Racist school, racist school!"'
- **h** In January 1975, the first edition of *Panther's Rapp* was published. It was a Panther Party newspaper designed 'to give a true picture that will represent the Polynesians' interests, and their true identity.'
- **i** In 1981, Panther members participated in the anti-Springbok tour protests.

Grouping information into key ideas: Version 2

This is similar to the activity on the previous page, but is more challenging as there are THREE main ideas to figure out and group the information (**a** – **m**) into.

2 ACTIVITY

Read through the information below and highlight/identify any common words or ideas. Organise these into three groups. Write the letters into the boxes below. Write an appropriate 'label'.

Label 1:	**Label 2:**	**Label 3:**
Information Group 1:	**Information Group 2:**	**Information Group 3:**

a In late 1971, the Panthers carried out their first protest action, against a tour to South Africa by a men's softball team.

b In 1972 the Panthers participated in anti-Vietnam War protest marches.

c A Tenants' Aid Brigade was set up later in 1972 to help Pasifika people threatened with eviction *[removal]* from their rental properties.

d In 1974, several members travelled to Wellington to present submissions *[viewpoints]* on racism to the government.

e The Panthers were successful in getting traffic lights installed at a busy Ponsonby intersection where children were getting badly hurt.

f Panther member Tigi Ness recalled going out with the Police Investigation Group ('PIG patrol'): 'A group of us got together with some cars and some *Palagi* students who had cars; we went out to the Minister of Immigration's house. Three o'clock in the morning we were out there with loud hailers and spotlights, and shone them on his house. "Bill Birch, come out with your passport now!" When the lights went on and they all came out, we'd take off. Just to turn the tables; we knew where he lived.'

g In January 1975, the first edition of *Panther's Rapp* was published. It was a Panther Party newspaper designed 'to give a true picture that will represent the Polynesians' interests, and their true identity.'

h The Panthers supported the Maori Land March protest *[hikoi]* in 1975.

i In 1981, Panther members participated in the anti-Springbok tour protests.

j In response to the aggressive approach of the Police Task Force, the Panthers, in partnership with other groups, set up a Police Investigation Group (PIG), to monitor it. The PIG patrols followed the Task Force around, and handed out information to people on their legal rights.

k Tigi Ness was expelled from Mt Albert Grammar School in the early 1970s for refusing to cut his Afro: 'A lot of students from university heard I was being expelled, and the Polynesian Panthers had just been formed, so as I was leaving school the Panthers came up with placards and protested: "Racist school, racist school!"'

l The Panthers ran programmes to inform people of their rights under the law, especially if being questioned or arrested by the police.

m The Panthers helped with transport in the weekends for families who couldn't afford to visit their relatives in Paremoremo Prison.

TODAY IN HISTORY

OCTOBER

2/10/1839	Scotsman Kirkpatrick McWilliam invents the bicycle
3/10/1990	East and West Germany are reunited after 45 years of division during the Cold War
15/10/1993	New Zealand's first 'victim' of a speed camera is snapped, near Petone
22/10/1773	King of Tonga presents Captain Cook with a giant turtle, which dies in London Zoo in 1966
25/10/1920	King Alexander of Greece dies from blood poisoning after being bitten by a pet monkey

ISBN: 9780170352581

Grouping information into key ideas: Extension

Below is some information that you have found during an inquiry about Tonga. You realise that there is a bit too much information to cram into one paragraph, so you think about how to sensibly divide it into FOUR groupings of common ideas (paragraphs).

3 ACTIVITY

1 Read through the information below (**a** – **w**) and **highlight/identify any common words/ideas/ types of actions that could be grouped together**.

2 Come up with a 'label' for each grouping, and then write the letter of each piece of information into the appropriate box below.

Label 1:	**Label 2:**	**Label 3:**	**Label 4:**
Information Group 1:	**Information Group 2:**	**Information Group 3:**	**Information Group 4:**

a A Treaty of Friendship between Tonga and Britain was signed in 1900.

b Queen Salote married in 1917 and ascended to the throne the following year when her father, King George Tupou II, died.

c Less than a year after they arrived in Tonga, the American troops had mostly gone, and 2000 New Zealand troops replaced them, maintaining a military presence.

d At the top of Tongan society was a class of titleholders or rulers, including the nobles (*nopele*) and the King.

e Relationships between the different classes had for centuries been a powerful form of social control in Tonga, especially between the nobles and the commoners.

f Like Britain's Queen Victoria almost a century earlier, Salote was only 18 when she became Queen: she would, the nobles thought, be easy to manipulate *[control]*.

g At the end of the 20th century, the King (along with the nobles) controlled 70 percent of the seats in Tonga's Parliament.

h For its own defence during World War Two, Tonga raised an army of 2700 men, with 50 of these serving in the Fijian battalion in the Solomons. One was killed, three were wounded and five received bravery medals.

ISBN: 9780170352581

- **i** The bulk of the people in Tonga were the commoners (*tu'a*).
- **j** Like other Allied places, Tonga also experienced an American 'invasion' during World War Two, with over 9000 soldiers arriving in May 1942 to defend the Pacific.
- **k** Tonga's stable form of government meant that, unlike virtually every other Pacific Island nation in the 19th century, Tonga alone had avoided being formally *[officially]* annexed *[taken over]* by a foreign power.
- **l** Medical centres were established by US soldiers, and campaigns to reduce the impact of flies, mosquitoes, fleas and rats were carried out.
- **m** Salote Mafile'o Pilolevu Tupou III, or Queen Salote (Charlotte), was born in 1900, and later attended school for five years in Auckland.
- **n** Experts in Tongan traditions (*matapule*) were next most important in rank, followed by skilled craftsmen (*mua*).
- **o** Tonga became a 'Protectorate of Britain' in 1899, and this gave British officials significant influence, although Tonga remained independent.
- **p** While in Tonga, US troops built 100 km of new roads, a runway and the Nuku'alofa wharf.
- **q** Queen Salote attended the 1953 coronation *[crowning]* of the young Queen Elizabeth II in London, and won over the spectators by choosing to be driven through the streets in an open carriage, smiling and waving, in the pouring rain.
- **r** Tonga's Treaty of Friendship remained in place until 1970, when Tonga and Britain parted on good terms.
- **s** The source of the King's power was the 1875 Constitution, which had entrenched *[embedded]* the King's authority over and above all others.
- **t** The Americans stationed in Tonga during the war were wealthy beyond anything Tonga had seen, and they were generous.
- **u** After 47 years on the throne, Queen Salote died in 1965, and her passing was mourned throughout Tonga. Her long reign *[rule]* was recognised as one of peace, unity and stability.
- **v** Relations between the US troops and the Tongan people were generally very good, although they began to deteriorate *[worsen]* as the war progressed and fear of a Japanese invasion declined.
- **w** Salote promoted education for girls and stressed the value of the contribution of women, although she placed an emphasis on their traditional roles (they did not get the right to vote until 1960).

FINISHED?

How many of each type of 'hard' fact are there in this information? The different 'types' are: **names** (of people, places or events); **dates** of events; **statistics** (numbers); **short quotes** (from eyewitnesses and/or experts).

______________ / ______________ / ______________ / ______________

Discuss your findings with the class.

 ISBN: 9780170352581

11 Paragraph topic sentences

When writing an essay, your ideas and information will come from your inquiry and/or class notes. You will still need to organise them into kete or groups that focus on one main point. There is almost always more than one way to group these ideas, so choose one that makes sense to you and will be easy for the reader to understand. Once you have sorted your ideas into groups, you can write topic sentences that sum up what that group of ideas is about.

1 ACTIVITY

Remembering that a *topic sentence* introduces the *one main idea* in a paragraph, choose the ONE appropriate topic sentence for the information given.

<table>
<tr><th colspan="2">Possible topic sentences</th><th>Information on the one main idea</th></tr>
<tr><td>1</td><td>Most people spend about a third of their lives asleep.</td><td rowspan="4">Apples are pip fruit.
Oranges are citrus fruit.
Peaches and nectarines are called stone fruit.
Even tomatoes are actually fruit!
Different types of fruit grow best in different countries.</td></tr>
<tr><td>2</td><td>Youths in Palestine threw rocks and fruit at Israeli soldiers.</td></tr>
<tr><td>3</td><td>There are many different types of fruit.</td></tr>
<tr><td>4</td><td>A healthy diet contains fruit and vegetables.</td></tr>
</table>

Although this is a very basic example, it should illustrate the idea that a topic sentence is like a shop sign that tells people as they walk down the street what that shop is all about; in other words, what sort of products it sells. Just as it would be silly for a fruit and vegetable shop to put out a sign advertising shoes, when we write our paragraphs we want to 'advertise' in our topic sentences the main point that is actually inside the body of the paragraph. Hopefully, you chose number 3!

2 ACTIVITY

Below is a bunch of information you've discovered while following Bob on Facebook.

You've decided to write an essay that responds to this simple topic: 'What things does Bob enjoy?'

Rather than just talk about all the things below in one big, random paragraph, you decide, after looking carefully at the information, that THREE paragraphs would make sense. This is because there seems to be three main types of things that Bob enjoys.

1 Identify the three main types of things that Bob enjoys.
2 Write a topic sentence that uses important words from the essay topic above, AND identifies which type of things Bob enjoys that you will talk about.

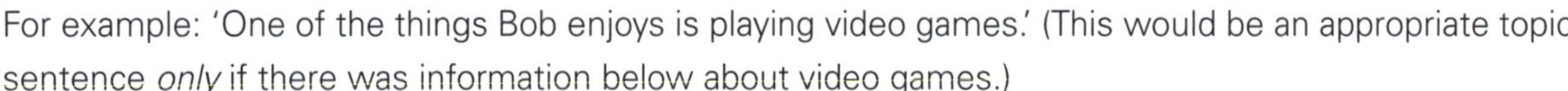

For example: 'One of the things Bob enjoys is playing video games.' (This would be an appropriate topic sentence *only* if there was information below about video games.)

- **a** Bob really likes Granny Smith apples.
- **b** Bob watches at least two hours of TV every night, more on the weekends.
- **c** Bob kayaked on the nearby lake one weekend with his friends.
- **d** For Bob, *South Park* is still a favourite.
- **e** Whenever Bob can find them at the shop, Bob buys pineapples.
- **f** Bob makes sure he's home from whatever he's doing in time to watch *Shortland Street*.
- **g** Bob plays rugby league for his school team on the weekends.
- **h** Bob loves grapes, even though they usually are imported ones.
- **i** Bob's had a go at kilikiti, and even though he wasn't very good, he thought it was fun.
- **j** Bob always puts the sound on mute when the ads come on TV.
- **k** Bob enjoys bananas, especially if they've been barbecued.
- **l** Bob loves snorkelling, especially at the local marine reserve.

What Bob enjoys 1	What Bob enjoys 2	What Bob enjoys 3
Topic sentence, paragraph 1	**Topic sentence, paragraph 2**	**Topic sentence, paragraph 3**

 ISBN: 9780170352581

3 ACTIVITY

You may not know much about the information on the right-hand side of this table, but don't be put off. You should still be able to choose the ONE topic sentence from the left-hand side that best sums it up.

	For each of questions 1–4, circle the number of the best topic sentence below ...	... that covers as much of this information as possible.
1	**a** Many people do not care what a government does. **b** Some governments pay for fire-fighting and surf lifesaving. **c** In a democracy, we are free to elect our own government. **d** The government should make the laws, keep the peace, and provide free education. **e** People have different expectations about what a government should do.	• Some people believe that the government does not have the right to interfere in their lives very much at all. • Most people believe that the government should protect the country from invasion. • Most people want the government to provide education for children. • Many people do not like to pay taxes, but still expect the government to provide services.
2	**a** Totalitarian governments can be communist or fascist. **b** There are a number of different ideas about how governments should operate. **c** Democracy is the best type of government. **d** There are many countries that are still not democratic. **e** Governments rule people.	• A fascist government is one with a strong ruler, or dictator. • A communist government believes people should share wealth equally. • A democratic government believes that the people should be free to make choices. • In a theocracy, the government rules according to religious laws.
3	**a** In a democracy, there are elections to make sure the people have their say. **b** Communism and fascism are different to democracy. **c** In Nazi Germany, there was a fascist dictatorship. **d** There are often said to be two main ideologies of government: left-wing and right-wing. **e** It is important that people in a democracy do not let a dictator gain power.	• Voting is secret in a democracy so that it is safe to vote against the government. • Unlike under fascism, in a democracy elections are held to choose the government people want. • Unlike under communism, in a democracy the media is not controlled by the government, and can criticise it. • The government does not control sports or social clubs in a democracy.
4	**a** Communism spread from Russia to other parts of the world. **b** Communist governments were all imposed on their peoples, rather than being elected to power. **c** Communism was seen as a great threat to Western democratic values. **d** Between 1917 and 1961, there were many revolutions around the world. **e** Communism as a system of government had collapsed in Europe by 1990.	• After World War Two, many of the countries of Eastern Europe became communist. • The first country to 'turn communist' was Russia, after the 1917 revolution. • Communism spread to Asia after Mao Zedong's forces were victorious in the civil war that ended in 1949. • In 1961, Cuba was the first (and only) country to become communist in the 'western hemisphere'.

ISBN: 9780170352581

4 ACTIVITY

Below, in the left-hand column, is some information you've found in an inquiry. It helps to answer this question:

What were relations like between Maori and Pakeha in the early times of contact?

Here's the information you've found to go into a paragraph.	**In a few words of your *own*, summarise briefly what this information is about.**	**Turn those few words into a sentence … a topic sentence!** *Remember to use the most important words from the question above.*
• Maori were keen to get hold of European technology such as muskets (guns). • Europeans were keen to get Maori permission — and help — to cut flax and timber (for sale in Europe). • Maori would supply European ships with food in return for trade goods.		
• Missionaries believed that Maori needed to be 'saved' by converting them to Christianity. • The first mission station was established in 1814 in the Bay of Islands; more were soon established nearby. • Missionaries tried to stop Maori cultural practices such as cannibalism, tattooing and slavery.		
• By 1840, Maori were becoming concerned about European troublemakers. • European whalers in Northland often got drunk and caused fights. • Maori liked the idea of British officials stepping in, but only to control British people.		

ISBN: 9780170352581

12 Paragraph structure activities

1 ACTIVITY

Review the paragraph structure (TEE) section, pages 92–93.

The paragraphs in the table below on the Pasifika migration experience have the topic sentences separated out.

1 Read the 'Explanation and Examples' section and write the correct topic sentence from the selection of topic sentences (in the box) below in the appropriate space.

2 Identify the 'hard' facts (Examples) in the second column by highlighting them. (Refer to pages 28 and 94 for a reminder of what are 'hard' facts.)

Selection of topic sentences

A The Polynesian Panther Party (PPP) was formed by the Tongan Will 'Ilolahia to help out those who were struggling.

B The second area of concern that the Panthers wanted to address was education.

C Young Pasifika people growing up in New Zealand in the 1970s found themselves having to live in two very different worlds.

D The third key goal of the Panthers was to unite with like-minded groups, both brown and white.

E Young Pasifika people in the 1970s responded differently to the racism they experienced.

F There were three key areas of concern that the Polynesian Panther Party wanted to address, and the first of these was racism.

G Pasifika peoples were encouraged to come to New Zealand in the 1960s, but in the following decade the mood changed to a more negative one.

Topic sentence	Explanation and Examples ('hard' facts)
	During the 1960s, many Pacific Island people were encouraged to migrate to New Zealand due to an industrial *[factory]* labour shortage in this country. By the 1970s, as economic conditions worsened, calls came from different sectors of New Zealand society to stop immigration from the Pacific. In 1975, the National government looked at the idea of deporting *[sending back]* law-breaking immigrants. This shows that in some people's minds, immigration was linked to crime. Immigration regulations, and the policing of them, were tightened. This negative view of Pasifika peoples was challenged by a range of groups opposed to racism, most notably the Polynesian Panthers.

ISBN: 9780170352581

Topic sentence	Explanation and Examples ('hard' facts)
	One was the world of their parents, which revolved around family and church, and had strong connections back to the home islands. These included Tonga, Samoa, and the Cook Islands. The other was the New Zealand world, which was still mostly monocultural (European). This world found it difficult to accept these new New Zealanders who were so different to them. Racist attitudes towards Pasifika people were not uncommon. A common term of abuse was 'coconut'.
	Pasifika girls tended to 'internalise' *[lock inside]* their feelings, and they tried to be 'invisible', at least when Europeans were around. Young men, in contrast, might respond by lashing out physically, especially once they were beyond the influence of home and church. For some, involvement in gangs (such as the Mongrel Mob and Hells Angels) and crime could follow. For others, however, the situation of Pasifika people became a reason to take action against the discrimination. They were usually those who had already had some experience with the 'European system'. Often this was through acting as interpreters for their parents in their dealings with officials, such as in schools.
	'Ilolahia was a former gang member with the 'Nigs'. He gradually came to the realisation that his gang lifestyle had no future. Instead, he turned to education and political awareness as a means to help not just himself, but also other young Pasifika people who were heading into trouble. This worked, and the PPP attracted a number of young people, most around of them around 18. They were from Tongan, Samoan, and Cook Island backgrounds, as well as Maori.
	According to former Panther member Melani Anae, two *Papalagi* (Pakeha New Zealander) groups identified as particularly in need of greater awareness were the police and landlords. More generally, the Panthers wanted to overcome the negative views that many *Papalagi* had, to make them realise, as Anae explained, 'that we weren't just robbers and rapists, as the media was putting out there; that we were just migrants and their New Zealand-born children, dealing with issues of settlement (for our parents) and identity (for the youth).'
	To help out young students with their school work, Panther members who were at university set up the first community homework centre in Ponsonby. While promoting the value of education as a means to get ahead was vital, just as important was to foster *[grow]* pride in Pasifika heritage. This message was similar to the American black nationalists' motto of 'Black Pride'.
	The aim was to work together on issues that concerned all poor and marginalised peoples, even if the Panthers themselves were generally focused on Pasifika peoples. On this basis, the Panthers worked closely with Nga Tamatoa, the organisation of Maori university students, and the Peoples' Union. The Panthers also reached out to the gangs, such as Black Power and Mongrel Mob, as some of the older members were once in them.

 ISBN: 9780170352581

2 ACTIVITY

You may not be familiar with this content, but the TEE paragraph structure remains the same.

Process

1 Highlight what you think are the key words in the topic sentence in the table below (see the example).
2 Try to find similar words in the 'Explanation' column — highlight them.
3 Finally, try to find some 'hard' facts in the third column, which back up and 'prove' the topic sentence true. For example (see highlighting below): **A** = **3** = **g**.

Topic sentence	Explanation	Evidence/'hard' facts
A In the 1840s, both the Governor and Maori chiefs acted as though they each had the right to make laws and rule in New Zealand.	**1** Maori centred on the Waikato region set up their own European-style Maori King in order to control sale of their lands.	**a** A total of 3.5 million acres was confiscated *[taken]*: over 1.2 million in the Waikato and nearly 1.3 million in Taranaki. Some tribes who had not even fought had land taken.
B The newly arriving settlers were promised plenty of cheap land by the New Zealand government.	**2** The Pakeha government decided to crush the Kingitanga by force. After many battles, the Maori resistance was finally broken.	**b** In all, up to 18,000 full-time British soldiers were fighting about 5000 Maori 'part-time' fighters. The main battles were at Rangiriri (Waikato) and Gate Pa (near Tauranga).
C By the late 1850s, the settlers began to demand the right to rule themselves.	**3** The Governor passed several laws affecting Maori, while the chiefs continued to rule over their own tribes.	**c** In the North Island (Auckland region), 40 acres of land were sometimes given to each adult settler, and 20 acres for each child. By 1860, 65 percent of Maori land was owned by settlers.
D In the late 1850s, some Maori decided to take political action to prevent sales of their remaining land.	**4** The settlers wanted their own Parliament so that they could make the laws, rather than have the Governor make the laws.	**d** By the 1880s, the population had dropped to a low of about 42,000. Tuberculosis, diphtheria and influenza killed many Maori. Over 90 percent of Maori lived in isolated rural areas. They owned just 12 percent of the land they had owned in 1840.
E The Pakeha government saw the Kingitanga as unlawful and decided to take military action against it.	**5** Maori had lost much of their land through sales and confiscations, and as a result were poor, unhealthy and had poor housing.	**e** In 1852, Britain approved a law (the Constitution Act) that gave the New Zealand settlers their own Parliament. Most Maori were not included in it. However, section 71 of the Act allowed for districts where Maori rule was to remain, but this was ignored.

Table continues on page 108

ISBN: 9780170352581

Topic sentence	Explanation	Evidence/'hard' facts
F After the wars, the government passed laws that confiscated *[took]* large areas of Maori land.	**6** Many settlers were attracted to New Zealand by the offer of cheap land, which they began farming within a short space of time. Maori were at first keen to sell.	**f** This movement began in the Waikato and was called the Kingitanga. The first Maori King was appointed in 1857, and his name was Te Wherowhero. When he died two years later, his son Tawhiao became King.
G By 1900, Maori were marginalised *[outcasts]* on the edge of Pakeha society.	**7** The confiscations were supposed to punish the 'rebels' for their unlawful actions. Maori iwi that were affected protested that the confiscation laws were illegal.	**g** One of the laws that Governor Hobson passed forbid Northland Maori to cut down any more kauri trees. Local chiefs, such as Hone Heke, ignored this law. Another law was a tax on imported goods.

How many 'hard' facts are there in total in the third column? Highlight them in a different colour. These could be:

- names (of people, places, events and organisations)
- dates of events
- statistics (numbers)
- short quotes from people such as eyewitnesses or experts.

Total number of 'hard' facts (in the third column) =

When finished, discuss your total with your classmates.

TODAY IN HISTORY

NOVEMBER

1/11/1512 Michelangelo's paintings on the ceiling of the Sistine Chapel in Rome are first exhibited
2/11/1902 Sydney bather William Gocher arrested at Manly for wearing a swimsuit in daylight
3/11/1792 Building begins on first European dwelling in New Zealand, a 12 x 5.5 m bunkhouse for a sealing party left at Dusky Sound
4/11/1922 Entrance to King Tutankhamen's tomb discovered in Egypt
5/11/1605 Guy Fawkes arrested in 'Gunpowder plot' to blow up the British parliament
10/11/1868 Te Kooti's men kill 70 Pakeha and Maori loyalists at Matawhero
11/11/1918 Armistice signed ending WWI at 11 am
15/11/1861 *Otago Daily Times* established as New Zealand's first daily paper
17/11/1869 Suez Canal opens, linking the Mediterranean and Red Seas
22/11/1963 President Kennedy assassinated while travelling in a motorcade through Dallas, Texas
28/11/1979 Air New Zealand DC-10 crashes into Mt Erebus in Antarctica, killing 257

ISBN: 9780170352581

3 ACTIVITY

You may not be familiar with the content below, but that won't matter.

1 Use the following sets of '**Paragraph Information**' (right side) to choose the ONE best topic sentence from the '**Possible topic sentences**' box (left side). **Hint**: As you read the paragraph information, try to think of what is the one main idea being talked about.

2 Circle the topic sentence number and in the space below write a brief one-sentence explanation of why you chose it.

Topic A: Conflict in Ireland

Possible topic sentences	Paragraph 1: Information
A Ireland is a country often called the 'Emerald Isles' because it is a very beautiful country and it has experienced conflict. **B** The main reason why England tried to extend its rule over Ireland from the 12th century was a fear of attack through Ireland from other Catholic countries like Spain and France. **C** Differences over religion, culture and control of political and economic power caused conflict in Ireland. **D** The northern part of Ireland was the first main area to come under British control in order to avoid conflict. **E** In Ireland there has been violent conflict between Catholics and Protestants.	• Irish Catholics resented past English efforts to crush their Gaelic culture. • Many Irish Catholics disliked being controlled by the English Parliament. • In general, the descendants of the English Protestant settlers controlled the industrial wealth of the north of Ireland. • Most of the land in the south was owned by the Protestant English settlers, generally leaving Irish Catholics poor. • There were fewer employment opportunities in higher paying jobs for Irish Catholics, due to discrimination.

1 Explanation of your choice of topic sentence: ______________________

____

____

Possible topic sentences	Paragraph 2: Information
A By the end of the 19th century, there had been a long history of violent action against British control of Ireland. **B** Most Irish Catholics resented the way the English had tried to crush their culture, including their religion. **C** There were a number of different nationalist groups whose aim was to end, or at least limit, British control over Ireland. **D** Many Irish people favoured a peaceful and lawful approach to removing British control over Ireland. **E** Protestants in Ireland claimed that they had as much right to Ireland as the Catholics.	• Some Irish Catholics were impatient with the slow pace of reforms and wanted to use violence to rid Ireland of British influence. • One group of Irish Catholics believed that it was important to revive Ireland's own culture as a means to regaining self-belief and, eventually, political control. • Some of the people who were prepared to use violence secretly took key positions in Irish cultural groups. • Another group of Catholic Irish people believed that self-rule could be gained by working legally through the British Parliament.

ISBN: 9780170352581

2 Explanation of your choice of topic sentence: ____________________

____

____

Possible topic sentences	Paragraph 3: Information
A The British Army did not have the situation in Ireland under control if there were to be trouble between the rival groups.	• Irish Nationalist Party leader John Redmond and British Prime Minister Herbert Asquith were at first convinced that greater independence in Ireland would be accepted without trouble.
B Some said that the Unionists were unreasonable in their demand that Ireland should not receive greater political freedom.	• Pro-British Protestant Irish, backed by the Conservative opposition party in Britain, vowed to oppose 'by any means necessary' the loosening of British control over Ireland.
C The decision to grant Ireland greater political freedom intensified the conflict there as rival political groups began to arm themselves.	• In opposition to greater independence for Ireland, pro-British Irish Protestants set up their own private army, the Ulster Volunteer Force (UVF).
D Pro-British Protestants were genuinely concerned that the loosening of the political bonds with Britain would put them and their livelihoods in danger.	• In response to the UVF, Irish Catholics established their own private army, the Irish Volunteer Force (IVF), to ensure that the promised political freedom would still be granted. • A third private army, the Irish Citizen Army (ICA), was created by workers who wanted not just greater political freedom but a full revolution.
E The INP won the balance of power in the 1911 election and thus was able to get Liberal Party support for Home Rule in Ireland.	• The IVF and UVF built up supplies of weapons as the time drew nearer when the promised greater political freedom was due to be granted.

3 Explanation of your choice of topic sentence: ____________________

____

____

Possible topic sentences	Paragraph 4: Information
A The INP's desire for some authority in Ireland was finally granted and was due to take effect in 1914, despite the opposition of the House of Lords.	• There had been two previous unsuccessful political attempts for Irish Catholics to gain more control in their own country, but these were blocked by political opponents.
B The House of Lords' power of blocking a bill *[veto]* was reduced by a law supported by the INP.	• The Irish Nationalist Party (INP) won enough seats in the 1910 British election to form a government with the British Liberal Party.
C The Conservative Party had blocked two previous attempts at introducing greater political authority for Irish Catholics.	• Despite strong opposition from the British Conservative Party, the first steps were taken in 1911 to give Irish Catholics some independence from British rule.
D As 1914 approached, opposition to greater authority for Irish Catholics increased, with rival armies being set up in Ireland.	• In 1912, the British House of Lords tried to block greater independence for Irish Catholics, but only succeeded in delaying this process until 1914.
E The INP had gained the support of most Irish Catholics because of its policy of greater political power for Irish Catholics in Ireland.	

 ISBN: 9780170352581

4 Explanation of your choice of topic sentence: ______

______

______

Topic B: The end of World War One

Possible topic sentences	Paragraph 5: Information
A The peace treaty after World War One (WWI) was signed at Versailles. **B** Hitler had fought in World War One (WWI) and had been injured, but he survived and went on to become dictator of Nazi Germany. **C** The American President Wilson wanted a just peace after World War One (WWI). **D** Britain and France had similar ideas about how the treaty should be made. **E** The four main winning countries all had different ideas on the sort of treaty that should be made with Germany at the end of World War One (WWI). **F** The treaty with Germany was only one of several treaties signed between the victors and losers of World War One (WWI).	• France's leader Georges Clemenceau wanted a harsh peace treaty for revenge and also to ensure that Germany could 'never again' attack France. • Britain's Prime Minister Lloyd George had promised to 'squeeze Germany until the pips squeak' and to 'make them pay', but in reality he was willing to accept a more moderate peace settlement. • America's President Wilson wanted a fair and just peace settlement based on his '14 Point Plan'. This included a new 'League of Nations' to peacefully settle any future disputes. • Italy's Orlando wanted to make territorial gains from the peace settlement, as this had been promised by the Allies when Italy entered the war on their side.

5 Explanation of your choice of topic sentence: ______

______

______

Possible topic sentences	Paragraph 6: Information
A Germany is a country with several main rivers, one of which is the Rhine. **B** Germany lost land in Europe to France, Poland, Denmark, Belgium and Lithuania. **C** Under the terms of the Treaty of Versailles, Germany was punished militarily, financially, territorially and 'morally'. **D** Britain and France wanted a treaty that was backed up by American power. **E** The Treaty of Versailles was supposed to be based on Wilson's earlier 'Fourteen Points'. **F** Germany regarded the Treaty as a 'diktat', as they were not part of the negotiations and were forced to sign it against their will.	• Under Article 231, Germany had to accept all the moral blame for starting World War One (WWI). • Under Article 42, the area known as the Rhineland had to be demilitarised; no weapons of war were allowed in that territory. • Under Article 232, Germany was obliged to pay reparations *[the financial cost of the war]*. • Germany was not allowed to unite with its neighbouring German-speaking country Austria (*Anschluss*). • Germany had to disarm *[get rid of its military forces]* and give up its colonies as well as some of its European territory. • The League of Nations took over control of some German territory.

ISBN: 9780170352581

6 Explanation of your choice of topic sentence: ______________________________

____

____

Possible topic sentences	Paragraph 7: Information
A The terms of the Treaty of Versailles upset most Germans. **B** The terms of the Treaty of Versailles upset Germany and it only signed because it had no other choice. **C** Historians still debate whether or not the Treaty of Versailles was fair. **D** The terms of the Treaty of Versailles eventually led to the outbreak of World War Two (WWII). **E** The Germans were probably being unreasonable in complaining about the terms of the Treaty, as they had lost the war and could expect no less. **F** Excessive German pride may have been the main reason behind their complaints about the terms of the Treaty, and their reluctance to sign it.	• Germany resented the loss to Poland of territory from its eastern provinces. • Germany complained that it could not afford what it called crippling reparations *[payment to the Allies of the full cost of the war]*. • Germany still considered itself a significant European power and resented not being treated like one. • Germany did not like that it had no say in determining the terms of the Treaty. • Germans bitterly hated the idea of having to accept all the blame for causing the war. • The German Chancellor *[Prime Minister]* Scheidemann resigned rather than sign the Treaty. The German Parliament left it until the last moment before reluctantly agreeing to sign.

7 Explanation of your choice of topic sentence: ______________________________

____

____

Possible topic sentences	Paragraph 8: Information
A Germany claimed that the Treaty of Versailles was unfair for several reasons. **B** France claimed that the Treaty of Versailles was fair for several reasons. **C** Germany was still a large and powerful country after World War One (WWI). **D** Despite Germany's earlier harsh treaty with Russia, Russia thought that the Treaty of Versailles was *too* harsh. **E** France was determined to make Germany suffer at least as much as the Russians had under the 1917 Treaty of Brest-Litovsk.	• France claimed that Germany had started and then lost the war and must therefore face the consequences. • According to the French, Germany had forced a harsh treaty (Treaty of Brest-Litovsk) upon Russia in exchange for peace when it pulled out of the war back in 1917. • France pointed to the destruction Germany had caused as the major battles of World War One (WWI) had mostly been on French soil. • Germany was still a strong country and had to be weakened to prevent a future war, especially with its neighbour France.

8 Explanation of your choice of topic sentence: ______________________________

____

____

 ISBN: 9780170352581

Writing good topic sentences in response to an essay topic/question

Topic sentences are one of the most useful 'signposts' in an essay in terms of helping the reader follow your ideas. See *'Searching in books'*, page 12.

Here is an example of an essay topic/question:
'What actions were taken against different groups in Nazi Germany by the government?'

Step 1: Underline/highlight just the key words from the essay topic/question.
These are the **key words** you might underline. *You might decide that there are other important ones, too.*

'What actions were taken against different groups in Nazi Germany by the government?'

Step 2: Gather relevant information that helps to clearly respond to the essay topic/question.
You can find information through an inquiry or from your textbook. You'll need to organise it into groups of similar ideas to make it easy for the reader to follow your points.

Step 3: Write your topic sentences.
To be effective your topic sentences must do TWO things:

- **a** Use the **key words** that you've identified from the essay topic/question. This ensures that your paragraph will be clearly responding to the essay topic/question.
- **b** **Signal the main point** that the paragraph will be covering, in response to the essay topic/question.

An appropriate topic sentence for the above essay topic/question might look something like this:
'A main action taken against *Jews* in Nazi Germany by the government *was the Holocaust*.'

This topic sentence has:

1. Clearly used key words from the essay topic/question.
2. Clearly signalled the group *(Jews)* that had action taken against them *(the Holocaust)* in Nazi Germany.

TODAY IN HISTORY

DECEMBER

1/12/1955	Rosa Parks, a black woman from Montgomery, Alabama, is arrested for refusing to give up her bus seat for a white man
10/12/1868	World's first traffic lights begin operation off London's Parliament Square
17/12/1903	Orville and Wilbur Wright make first successful powered aeroplane flight in North Carolina
18/12/1916	Ten-month Battler of Verdun ends with 543,000 French and 434,000 German troops killed
21/12/1964	Last whale harpooned from a New Zealand ship
25/12/1818	*Silent Night* sung for the first time in Oberndorf, Austria
28/12/1869	American William Semple patents chewing gum
30/12/1835	Charles Darwin, the 'father of evolution', leaves New Zealand noting that it is 'not a pleasant place'

ISBN: 9780170352581

4 ACTIVITY

1 Underline the key words in the following essay topics/questions.

2 Use the bullet point information supplied for you to write an appropriate topic sentence.

HINT: where possible, try to think of a single key idea that sums up the information in the middle column, rather than just listing all the items there in your topic sentence.

Essay topic/Question	Information	Topic sentence
1 What methods did many southern states in America use to prevent blacks from voting up to the mid-1960s?	• Literacy tests • State laws • Terror and fear	
2 What actions did the black civil rights movement in America take during the 1950s and 1960s to bring about change?	• Montgomery bus boycott (non-violent) • Birmingham city non-violent protest marches • Selma city non-violent protest march	
3 What actions did the Black Panther Party take to help poor blacks in urban centres during the 1960s?	• Drug treatment programmes • Breakfast for Children programme • Free medical clinics • Adult education classes	
4 How did police in the South often respond to black civil rights protests during the 1960s?	• Police dogs • Beatings • Arrests • Water cannon	
5 What role did women typically play in the black civil rights movement of the 1960s?	• Participated in protests • Training others • Organising meetings • Advisors to protest leaders	
6 What official laws and rulings were the result of successful civil rights' actions after WWII?	• Desegregation of the military, 1948 • Supreme Court ruling ending segregated schooling, 1954 • Civil Rights Act, 1964 • Voting Rights Act, 1965	

ISBN: 9780170352581

FINISHED?

In the first column write your own essay topics/questions on a topic that you know or can easily research. In the second column provide three or four pieces of relevant bullet-pointed information. Swap these with a classmate who will write an appropriate topic sentence in the third column.

Essay topic/Question	Information	Topic sentence
1		
2		
3		

ISBN: 9780170352581

13 Paragraph critiquing and marking

The paragraph on the following page has been done as an example. You may not be familiar with the content, but that will actually be an advantage as you can focus on the following key points.

Point A: Does the topic sentence use *key words* from the essay question/topic to show clearly that it is answering it?

Point B: Does the topic sentence signal the *main point* that will be covered in the paragraph body, in response to what the essay question/topic has asked (without going into excessive detail)?

Point C: Does the explanation (and examples) in the main body of the paragraph focus on only the one main idea to be covered, as signalled in the topic sentence? (This will also keep the whole paragraph focused on what the essay question/topic has asked.)

Point D: Is there sufficient depth and detail to cover the paragraph's main idea well? If you find yourself having to ask questions about the paragraph content because you're not sure of something, then it is possible that the writer has not provided enough development of their points.

Point E: Are there good examples/'hard' facts to support the explanation? These could be any or all of:

- names (of people, places, events and organisations)
- dates of events
- statistics (numbers)
- short quotes from people such as eyewitnesses or experts.

ISBN: 9780170352581

Example

Essay focus question

What actions by aggressive powers increased tension in Europe and Asia between 1931 and 1937?

The 'hard' facts have been highlighted (only the first time they are used) to help with **Point E**.

It would have been good to include an example of the 'deep problems of the Great Depression', for example unemployment numbers.

Why didn't Britain and France want to offend Mussolini? [So he wouldn't be pushed into an alliance with Hitler.] This really should be explained.

A name [he was Emperor Haile Selassie] would have been good as a 'hard' fact here.

An aggressive action that increased tension in Europe and East Asia was the invasion of Abyssinia by Italy. Mussolini, the leader of Italy, wanted to divert Italians' attention away from the deep problems of the Great Depression by invading Abyssinia. Mussolini invaded without a declaration of war. Britain and France were not happy about the invasion of Abyssinia but did not want to offend Mussolini. Britain and France signed the Hoare-Laval Pact, agreeing that Mussolini could have parts of Abyssinia. The leader of Abyssinia, however, had fled the country and leaked the agreement to the newspapers. When the British public found out, they saw the Pact as an act of betrayal and forced some economic sanctions (punishments) to be applied to Italy.

This topic sentence is reasonably good for **Point A**, although the date of the invasion [it was 1935] would have shown that this 'aggressive action' was in the timeframe given in the focus question. **Point B** has been done well.

It would have been good to provide some sort of 'hard' fact here, such as the name of the region (even 'northern part' would do) or perhaps a percentage or area of land.

Examples of these 'economic sanctions' would be good [restrictions were eventually placed on selling metals and rubber to Italy].

Analysis comment for:

Point A: The topic sentence does use key words from the essay question/topic, although perhaps including the date of the invasion would show that this event is within the timeframe of the question.

Point B: The topic sentence does signal well the main point that is covered in the paragraph body: '*the invasion of Abyssinia by Italy*'. It doesn't go into unnecessary detail, leaving that for the main body of the paragraph — good!

Point C: All of the paragraph's explanation and examples are related to the one main idea as signalled in the topic sentence ('*the invasion of Abyssinia by Italy*').

Point D: There is reasonable depth and detail, although it would have been good if there was further explanation of some key points, as noted.

Point E: The supporting examples/'hard' facts are satisfactory, but there are areas as noted where they could have been improved, to make the paragraph stronger.

Overall comment: This is a reasonable paragraph with generally good structure. Where it is somewhat weak is in the explanation/examples: both needed to be developed further.

Your turn!

ISBN: 9780170352581

1 ACTIVITY

Essay focus question

What actions by aggressive powers increased tension in Europe and Asia between 1931 and 1937?

Paragraph 1

Another aggressive action taken by Germany that threatened peace in Europe and Asia was the attempt to unify with Austria (*Anschluss*). Germany attempted *Anschluss* with Austria. Hitler overestimated his power and sent troops to Austria. Italy was not happy about this and sent troops to the border of Italy and Austria. Germany then backed down. Hitler then in response to this rearmed and announced the existence of the *Luftwaffe*. Other countries then responded to this by preparing themselves for defence, not attack. France later built the Maginot Line in the hope that it would prevent the Germans from invading.

Your analysis comment for:

Point A: ______________________________

____

Point B: ______________________________

____

Point C: ______________________________

____

Point D: ______________________________

____

Point E: ______________________________

____

Overall comment: ______________________________

____

____

Paragraph 2

Japan invaded the Chinese province of Manchuria in 1931 in response to an 'alleged' attack on a Japanese railway station. Japan was quickly becoming overpopulated and saw Manchuria as a valuable source of raw materials, as well as an ideal place for population resettlement. The Japanese government was not told of the military action. China appealed to the League of Nations, asking them to condemn Japan as an aggressor. The League of Nations sent the Lytton Commission to investigate, headed by Lord Lytton (Britain). Lytton interviewed

 ISBN: 9780170352581

many people and went to the place where the supposed 'bombing' of the railway station had occurred. Eventually, Japan was declared the aggressor by the Commission, although no trade or economic sanctions (punishments) were applied. Angered, Japan withdrew from the League in 1933. Unstopped, Japan continued to expand into China and by 1937 had occupied coastal and other large areas of China moving towards the south.

Your analysis comment for:

Point A: ____________________

Point B: ____________________

Point C: ____________________

Point D: ____________________

Point E: ____________________

Overall comment: ____________________

Paragraph 3

Another action that led to tension in Europe was Germany's rearmament. A disarmament conference was held in 1932 for countries to discuss ways in which they could disarm. France was uneasy about Germany's presence and the tensions between the two led to Hitler leaving the conference and withdrawing from the League. Hitler then began to rearm at great speed. According to the Treaty of Versailles, Germany was only allowed an army of 100,000 men, no conscription and no air force (among other conditions). In 1935, Hitler announced that he had created a new German *Luftwaffe [air force]* and had introduced conscription to bring his army to 500,000 men. Both these actions were against the Treaty of Versailles and threatened peace in Europe.

Your analysis comment for:

Point A: ____________________

ISBN: 9780170352581

Point B: ______________________________

____

Point C: ______________________________

____

Point D: ______________________________

____

Point E: ______________________________

____

Overall comment: ______________________________

____

____

Paragraph 4

While all eyes were focused on Abyssinia, Hitler took yet another aggressive move. He occupied the Rhineland. This was a direct breach of the Locarno Pact of 1925 and the Treaty of Versailles, which stated that the Rhineland must remain demilitarised *[no weapons allowed]*. Hitler's reason for doing this was simple. He wanted to see if Britain and France would stop him. He wanted to know how far he could push them. His gamble paid off. The French offered no resistance and Germany overran the Rhineland. The unification of all German people had begun. Next, Japan slowly took over the province of Manchuria in China, which they renamed Manchukuo. Finally, in 1937, Japan began a full invasion of China. This, again, threatened peace in Europe and increased the already building tensions.

Your analysis comment for:

Point A: ______________________________

____

Point B: ______________________________

____

Point C: ______________________________

____

Point D: ______________________________

____

Point E: ______________________________

____

ISBN: 9780170352581

Overall comment: ______________________________

____

____

Essay focus question

What did the leaders of the 1916 Easter Rising in Ireland hope to achieve?

Paragraph 1

In the 1916 Easter Rising, only a handful of Irish 'rebel' leaders were actually informed of the rebellion, and the main backer of the rebellion was Patrick Pearse, leader of the revolutionary 'Fenians', otherwise known as the Irish Republican Brotherhood (IRB). It was Pearse's hope that the rebellion would bring a fully independent Ireland, free from British control. His idea was that in order for their country to be free, people (in this case, the rebels) would have to sacrifice their lives for Ireland, with hope that an emotionally driven Irish public would remember their cause and fight radically for an Irish republic. This idea was known as, in Pearse's own words, a 'blood sacrifice'. Pearse also planned such a rebellion to take place during Easter, an important time for Catholics in which they remember the resurrection of Jesus. Through the significance of the occasion, he hoped it would also symbolise the resurrection or rebirth of an independent Irish republic.

Your analysis comment for:

Point A: ______________________________

____

Point B: ______________________________

____

Point C: ______________________________

____

Point D: ______________________________

____

Point E: ______________________________

____

Overall comment: ______________________________

____

____

ISBN: 9780170352581

Paragraph 2

Patrick Pearse, who was the leader of the 1916 Easter uprising, hoped that the planned date of Easter Sunday would create a patriotic feeling amongst the Irish and they would rise up against the British. However, the ship the *Aud*, which was carrying 20,000 obsolete *[outdated]* German rifles for the uprising, was captured and sunk by the British. Also, the soldiers that Pearse was relying on using, the Irish Volunteers, had been told by their own leader not to support the Rising. Patrick Pearse and the other rebel military leaders realised that the Uprising would not have much success and the planned date of Easter Sunday was postponed until Easter Monday. Pearse decided to use yet another of the small Irish military groups that were opposed to British rule. James Connelly's Irish Citizen Army and Pearse's Irish Republican Brotherhood finally set out on their own to fight the British on Easter Monday. Because both armies were small and hopelessly outnumbered by the British, the Military Council came up with the idea of a 'blood sacrifice'. It was hoped that many of the soldiers would die for the cause and create a wave of support around Ireland for their cause.

Your analysis comment for:

Point A: ______________________________

____

Point B: ______________________________

____

Point C: ______________________________

____

Point D: ______________________________

____

Point E: ______________________________

____

Overall comment: ______________________________

____

____

____

ISBN: 9780170352581

Paragraph 3

James Connolly, leader of the Irish Citizen Army (ICA) during the 1916 Easter Rising, wanted Ireland not only to be free of British rule but also free of class divisions. Connolly had returned from the United States in 1910 committed to improving the poor conditions of the Irish workers, made worse, as he saw it, by 'British greed'. To carry out this fight, he became General Secretary of the Irish Transport and General Workers Union in 1914, as well as leader of the ICA. The ICA believed in violence as a necessary means to achieving an Irish republic. Like the Irish Republican Brotherhood, led by Patrick Pearse, this was a militia of active revolutionaries, and with just 220 men. Connolly, however, did not agree with Pearse's belief in a pointless 'blood sacrifice'. He believed in a full Marxist revolution. 'Governments are nothing more than committees of the rich,' he said. In January 1916, Connolly finally agreed to join with Pearse in the rebellion. In terms of military goals, it was hoped that the soldiers would be able to capture key places around Dublin, such as Dublin Castle (the British headquarters) and Bollands Mill, which would make it harder for the British soldiers to crush the uprising.

Your analysis comment for:

Point A: ______________________________

____

Point B: ______________________________

____

Point C: ______________________________

____

Point D: ______________________________

____

Point E: ______________________________

____

Overall comment: ______________________________

____

____

____

ISBN: 9780170352581

14 Essay introductions (and conclusions)

Below is a reminder of essay structure. Note how the introduction tells the reader briefly what is coming up in all of the essay's paragraphs (for *both* parts of the essay question/topic). You might also notice how this is very similar to what the topic sentence does for the paragraph: it introduces or signals the main point coming up in the paragraph body.

You have already done the series of activities to group similar information together and then write a topic sentence that sums up the one main idea. This is, in effect, the planning part of essay writing, where you sort your ideas (from your learning on the topic) into 'kete' or 'baskets' of similar information. Those kete become the basis of your paragraphs, and the one main idea for each kete/paragraph becomes the basis of your topic sentences (see *Essay structure*, page 89).

The easiest way to write your introduction is to take all of these topic sentences and group them together, one after the other. (You may need to rewrite them a bit so that the collected 'bunch' of topic sentences reads well.)

Note how all of the topic sentences for the first part of the essay question/topic become the first part of the introduction, and then these points are immediately followed by all of the topic sentences for the second part of the essay question/topic. (Again, you may need to do some rewriting so that the introduction reads well.)

The same applies for writing your conclusion. As you get better at this, you can write with more style, but it's always good to get the basics in place first before applying your own individual touch.

To summarise

From your planning, you can identify the main points that you want to make in response to the essay question/topic. From these main points you can write your topic sentences, and from *these* you have everything you need to write your introduction (and conclusion).

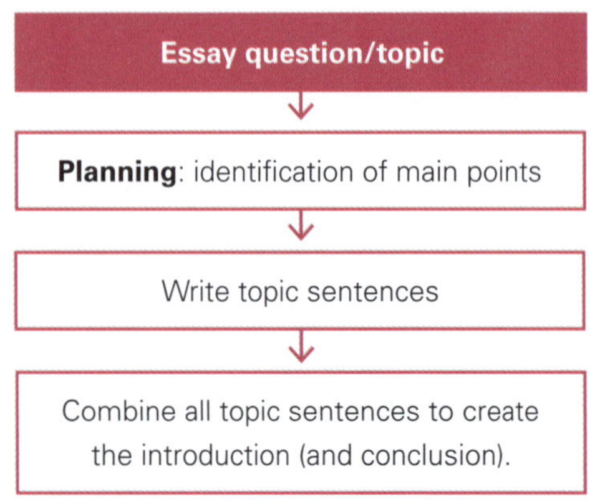

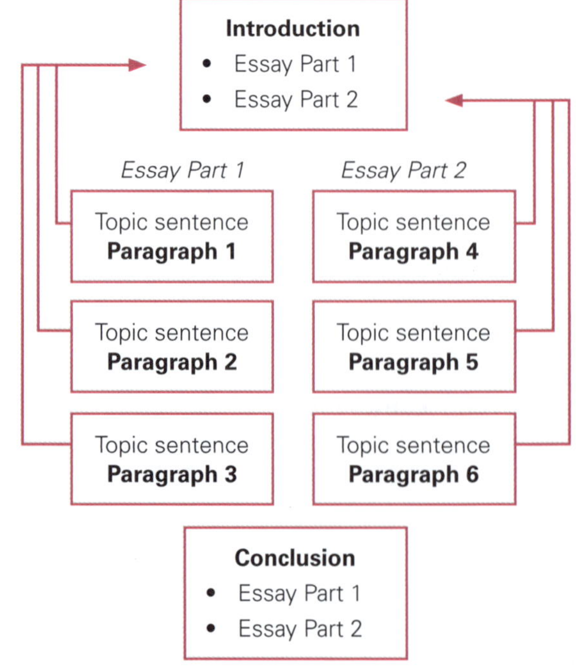

ISBN: 9780170352581

1 ACTIVITY

Introductions

While you can simply copy the topic sentences to create an introduction, the exercises below have taken the next step and reshaped them instead.

Refer to the 'TEE' paragraph structure activities you did on pages 109–112. Reread the topic sentences that you selected for those activities for both the Ireland and World War One topics:

A Circle the ONE essay introduction below that *best* sums up the main ideas from your selection of topic sentences.

B For each of the introductions that you reject, provide some brief details of *what you would expect to read about* in an essay with that introduction.

Topic A: Conflict in Ireland — possible introductions (refer to the activities, pages 109–110)

1 There were a number of different nationalist groups within Ireland whose aim was to end, or at least limit, British political, economic and cultural dominance over Ireland. This aim was finally granted, despite fierce opposition within both Britain and Ireland, and the conflict intensified as rival armies were established.

2 The Irish Nationalist Party, led by John Redmond, assured British Prime Minister Herbert Asquith that granting Ireland greater political freedom would be accepted by all groups within Ireland. However, the British Conservative Party and Ulster Protestants were utterly opposed.

3 Irish nationalists all had the similar aim of reducing or ending British rule in Ireland, but they did not agree on how to do this. One group was prepared to use violence, while another wanted a full socialist revolution to end the oppression of the workers. The Irish Nationalist Party, on the other hand, was prepared to use peaceful means to achieve its goal.

4 The British Conservative Party supported Ulster Protestants in their stated aim of keeping British control of Ireland 'by any means necessary'. This went as far as forming an army, the Ulster Volunteer Force, when it seemed that Britain itself would reduce its political authority in Ireland.

5 Different groups in Ireland wanted to have more political freedom. When this was finally granted, rival armies soon formed.

ISBN: 9780170352581

Topic B: The end of World War One — possible introductions (refer to the activities, pages 111–112)

1 The Treaty of Versailles was an unfair peace treaty forced on Germany by the Allies. American President Woodrow Wilson had hoped for a fairer peace.

2 The Allied powers had different ideas on how to treat Germany after the war. Eventually, it was agreed that Germany would be punished in four main ways. This caused anger in Germany but some satisfaction in France.

3 Germany lost World War One and France was determined that Germany would pay. Because of this, there were several different punishments in the Treaty of Versailles.

4 One of the main goals of Britain was to have Germany's Navy weakened. In the end, Germany actually destroyed its own Navy, rather than have it fall into British hands. Germany believed that the Treaty of Versailles was too harsh, but France thought that it was fair.

5 Germany did not like the 'war guilt' clause of the Treaty of Versailles. Under Hitler, Germany set out to have the Treaty overturned.

2 ACTIVITY

Identify the essay topics from the introductions

If an essay introduction has been well written, you should be able to guess what the essay question/topic is without even seeing it. This is because a good introduction should:

1 use *key words* from the essay question/topic
2 signal what main points will be coming up in the essay, in response to the question/topic.

Read the introductions from a series of different essays below. You probably won't know what the information is about, but don't worry — your job is just to figure out the TWO-PART essay topic.

1 Identify (highlight) the key words that you think come from each of the two parts of the essay topic. Then write what you think each part of the essay topic is into the box beneath each introduction.
2 In a different colour, highlight what you think are the main points that the writer is going to talk about in each part of the essay. Then write what you think are the main points (key ideas) for each part of the essay into the second box beneath each introduction.

ISBN: 9780170352581

The first one has been done for you as an example.

Because this is in brackets it is probably not a main point.

Example

During the period 1937 to 1939, three key factors contributed to the outbreak of war in 1939; these were the appeasement policy followed by Britain and France, Germany's take-over of Austria, and Germany's invasion of Poland (with the help of the German-Soviet Non-Aggression Pact). Between 1939 and 1941, war spread in Asia, into the Pacific and throughout Western Europe and Russia.

Likely essay topic: Part 1	Likely essay topic: Part 2
Describe the key factors between 1937 and 1939 that led to the outbreak of war in 1939.	Describe how the war spread between 1939 and 1941.
Likely main points (key ideas)	**Likely main points (key ideas)**
• Appeasement policy of Britain + France • Germany's take-over of Austria • Germany's invasion of Poland	• Spread into Asia • Spread into the Pacific • Spread in Western Europe/Russia

Your turn!

Introduction 1

During the period 1931–37, Italy, Japan and Germany all made aggressive movements that threatened to break the peace. Japan invaded Manchuria, Italy invaded Abyssinia, and Germany continued to defy the Treaty of Versailles by remilitarising the Rhineland and rearming. Other countries and the League of Nations protested, but took no further effective measures to deal with the aggressive nations during this period.

Likely essay topic: Part 1	Likely essay topic: Part 2
Likely main points (key ideas)	**Likely main points (key ideas)**

ISBN: 9780170352581

Introduction 2

The peace settlement after World War One (WWI) caused ill feeling between Germany and the Allies because Germany felt that, as a major European power, it had been forced to accept a peace treaty that was humiliating and too harsh. Relationships between European countries improved between 1924 and 1929 because Germany, under Chancellor Stresemann, began to 'fulfil' the terms of the Treaty of Versailles, leading to a series of pacts and treaties that settled postwar differences.

Likely essay topic: Part 1	Likely essay topic: Part 2
Likely main points (key ideas)	**Likely main points (key ideas)**

Introduction 3

The leaders of the 1916 Easter Rising hoped to achieve a countrywide revolt against British rule that would lead to the formation of an Irish republic. As a result of the failed Easter uprising and the harsh response of General Maxwell, anti-British feeling in Southern Ireland grew, and a new political party and military group were formed to continue the struggle.

Likely essay topic: Part 1	Likely essay topic: Part 2
Likely main points (key ideas)	**Likely main points (key ideas)**

 ISBN: 9780170352581

Introduction 4

The civil rights movement struggled to obtain for African Americans the same basic economic, political and social rights that were guaranteed to all Americans in the Constitution. There were both moderate and radical groups engaged in the civil rights movement, from the non-violent Southern Christian Leadership Conference to the more radical Black Panther Party and Black Muslims.

Likely essay topic: Part 1	Likely essay topic: Part 2
Likely main points (key ideas)	**Likely main points (key ideas)**

Summary

1 Explain what the introduction to an essay does, and how it does it.

2 Why is it so important to include 'hard' facts in your essay paragraphs?

3 Explain the way in which a paragraph topic sentence is similar to an essay introduction.

ISBN: 9780170352581

15 Essay planning and writing summary

When preparing to write an essay

1 Underline the key words from the essay question/topic. Be sure that you understand what is required.
2 From your sources of information (for example an inquiry, classroom notes, etc.), highlight any information that might be useful for responding to the essay task.
   - Make sure that any information you select is relevant. Reread the essay question/topic!
3 Make it easy for the reader to follow your thinking by grouping similar bits of information together: these groupings will be your paragraphs.
   - There is no one right way to group your ideas, but some ways make it easier for the reader to follow your thinking than others.
   - There is no 'right' number of paragraphs. Your groups of similar ideas will determine how many paragraphs you will use. Two or three paragraphs for each essay part is a rough guide (plus introduction and conclusion) for a Level 1 essay.
4 Once you have your groupings, look for additional 'hard' facts to use as evidence/examples. These include:
   - names (of people, places, events and organisations)
   - short quotes from people such as eyewitnesses or experts
   - dates of events
   - statistics (numbers).
5 Finally, write your topic sentences for each paragraph.
   - Remember, your topic sentences must use words from the essay question/topic and signal to the reader what will be the main point in the paragraph.

Introduction

Summarise your collection of topic sentences into an introduction. Do this for both parts of the essay task, with the second part following straight on from the first. You will now have told the reader very briefly about all of the main points coming up in the main body of the essay.

- DON'T say, 'In this I will tell you about …' Instead, actually outline your response to the essay task (your key ideas/main points).
- DO be specific. For example, 'There are <u>three</u> main differences between …' rather than the vague/weak 'There are <u>many</u> differences between …'

Main body

Write a sequence of paragraphs that follow the TEE structure. Start with a good topic sentence, explain your point and back it up with plenty of evidence ('hard' facts).

Conclusion

Summarise the main points from your essay plan, just as you did for your introduction. However, rather than just copy your introduction, reword it a bit differently.

- DON'T introduce new ideas here that weren't in the main body (that's where they go).
- DON'T give your opinion on the issues (unless the question asks for it).

ISBN: 9780170352581

16 Annotated essay exemplar

Before you look at the essay exemplar below, here's an example of how *not* to write an introduction to an essay.

'The wars in New Zealand in the 1860s were terrible and I think that they weren't fair for the Maori who lost lots of their land. In this essay I will tell you about the outbreak of the wars in the Waikato and Tauranga and their causes. I will also tell you about the main battles that happened in the Waikato and at Tauranga.'

- **DON'T give your opinion, unless the question asks for it.**
- **DON'T write in the 'first person' ('I').**
- **DON'T start, 'In this essay I will tell you about …' Just respond to the question, giving your main points (see the exemplar below).**

Essay topic (you must answer *both* parts)

In your essay, you should:

- describe the *short-term* and *long-term* causes of the war in the Waikato and Tauranga.
- describe the consequences in terms of the main battles that took place in the Waikato and Tauranga.

Essay exemplar

Introduction

The outbreak of the wars in the Waikato and Tauranga were caused by many reasons. A main reason was the misunderstanding of what was signed in the Treaty of Waitangi and another the settlers' desire for Maori land. This led to many problems between Maori and the British settlers and resulted in war. The four main battles that happened were the Waikato invasion, Meremere, Rangiriri, Orakau and finished in Gate Pa of Tauranga.

Avoid vague statements. TWO main reasons are identified in the next sentence, so this should say '… caused by two main reasons'. Other than this, the introduction clearly responds to the questions, and the link between the Part 1 'causes' and Part 2 'consequences' is clear — *ka pai!*

Hone Heke led his Maori people to sign the Treaty in 1840, thinking that the British would govern the British people and the Maori would govern the Maori people. This, however, was not the case. Soon after the Treaty was signed, British people started to fly their own flags. Hone Heke saw this as an act of disloyalty to his mana. Hone Heke was not happy with this so he decided to chop the flag pole at Kororareka down. He did this many times to prove his point, to show how disrespected he felt.

This topic sentence needs to *use words from the essay question/topic*, but it *is* signalling the general direction of the paragraph, although it is not *directly* on topic. Could be better.

Apart from the points noted, this paragraph is not too bad; although some more details and 'hard' facts would improve it.

Avoid vague statements. How many times? [Four!]

ISBN: 9780170352581

Govenor Grey wanted to attack the Maori people by surprise but he did not have enough resources or troops to do this so he talked to the people back in London and told them that the Maori were going to attack and he had not enough troops to fight back and if they could send him some to defend them. The people in London did not send over troops because they thought there were enough. Governor Grey then started steam power and steam boats. This was to their advantage. It was an easy way to get supplies to the troops and an easier way to get troops there.

This topic sentence needs to *use words from the essay topic*. It's also too long, but it does signal the *general* direction of the paragraph. Could be better.

Good points, but they need to be more clearly linked to answering the essay topic, rather than just 'jumbled' in. There is a shortage of 'hard' facts.

The main battles during the wars were Waikato, Meremere, Rangiriri, Orakau and then finished at Gate Pa (Tauranga). In the Waikato, the British took over, forcing Maori to move, the closest place being Meremere. The British then attacked the Maori at Meremere forcing them to move again, this time to Rangiriri. The same happened in Rangiriri. This made Maori turn to a famous Maori Chief, Rewi Manapoto, to lead them to battle against the British. He led his people to Orakau to build a pa. The only problem with the pa was they built in a horrible location. It was way too close to the British frontline and the pa had no easy escape or any way to bring water or guns and bullets into the pa. The British won in this battle.

Reasonable topic sentence, although the battle at Gate Pa is not actually covered in this paragraph, so it shouldn't be mentioned in the topic sentence. It is also good to link the battles here to the 'causes' from Part 1. Could do better.

This has some good points, but there could have been more 'hard' facts used to describe the battles (for example number of warriors/troops; numbers killed and wounded; dates of the battles).

On 29 April 1864 at Gate Pa (Pukehinahina), the best battle for the Maori people took place. Even though their numbers had dropped dramatically, they still fought a hard battle. There were only 300 Maori fighting, and this included children and women. They were up against a massive British side of 1120 troops and 17 field guns. The Maori dug underground bunkers to survive the bombardment, which lasted from early morning until 4 pm. They then came out of these when the British attacked, taking them by surprise. This was a very good decision and it forced the British back from Gate Pa. The British lost eight out of nine officers, and one-third of the 120-strong storming party. As General Duncan said: 'We were well and truly beaten.' A Maori woman, Heni Pore (or Jane Foley), is remembered for giving water to a dying British officer, Colonel Booth.

This is a reasonable topic sentence, as we know that the paragraph will be about Gate Pa, but it hasn't used words from the essay topic very well. Again, a link to the Part 1 'causes' would be good. Could do better.

This is a much better paragraph body — the best in the whole essay. It has plenty of detail and 'hard' facts — tino pai! (excellent!) If the rest of the paragraphs had been like this, it would have been a strong essay.

 ISBN: 9780170352581

In conclusion I believe that there was no real outcome to these battles. The confiscation of nearly 3 million acres of land still happened, Parihaka was invaded in 1881, and the misunderstanding of the Treaty of Waitangi still goes on. Even to this day there is no perfect translation and I don't think there ever will be.

This is a terrible conclusion. It uses the first person and contains an unasked-for opinion: 'I believe that ...' — WRONG! We don't use 'I' and we don't give our opinion, unless the question asks for it. There is also new information in here (about the land confiscations and invasion of Parihaka). DO NOT include new information in the conclusion — it goes in the main body (if it is relevant). The conclusion should just be a summary of the main points (rather like the introduction — go back and look at it now).

Overall comment

Despite the weaknesses noted, there is some depth and structure apparent in this essay, possibly shifting it from a high Achieved into a low Merit grade. An Excellence essay would need more accurate structure and more depth and details, particularly in the response to the first part of the essay topic. In addition, apart from in the introduction, the link between the Part 1 'causes' and the Part 2 'consequences' is not made very clear, and this would also need to be improved upon.

Note: Graded exemplar essays are available on NZQA's website.

Essay marking codes

Below are some codes next to markers' comments that your teacher could write on your essay when giving you feedback. You can also use these comments to self-mark and help you with your writing.

Introduction	
I1	Directly 'answer' BOTH parts of the essay question/topic, as though you were responding to a full-answer style of question. Use *key words* from the essay question/topic AND signal what your *main ideas* are.
I2	You must introduce the second part of the essay question/ topic here as well.
I3	You've got too much detail in your introduction. *Condense* this information down to two or three broad, general statements. Put the detail into paragraphs in the main body.
Paragraph structure and content	
P1	Your *topic sentence* needs to more clearly show that it is *answering the essay question/topic* by using *key words* from it.
P2	Your *topic sentence* needs to signal the *one main idea* that you will be talking about in the paragraph. (Use your planning to guide this.)
P3	This information does not relate to the *one main idea* contained in your *topic sentence* — rewrite the topic sentence so that it covers this information too.
P4	You've shifted to a new main idea here that is not covered by your topic sentence: start a *new paragraph* (see P1 and P2).
P5	The essay question/topic did not ask you about this. Either omit it entirely or explain why you think it is relevant.
P6	Your ideas jump around here. Write them in a *logical sequence*.
P7	You need to show the *link* in this 'Consequences' part of the essay back to the 'Causes' outlined in the first part of the essay.
P8	Try to *balance your essay* better so that you are covering the 'Causes' and 'Consequences' parts roughly equally in terms of amount written.

Style and content	
S1	Do not use the 'first person' (I/we): always write in the more formal 'third person' (he/she/they/it).
S2	Avoid sweeping generalisations and/or 'waffle'. Be *precise* with your statements.
S3	*Clarify* the meaning of this long/confusing sentence — rewrite it properly.
S4	Avoid slang/informal or emotive/exaggerated language.
S5	You've raised a good issue here. *Develop* it in order to tell the reader more about it.
S6	Explain this *detail* (even if briefly); the reader may not be sure of its significance.
S7	Provide a *'hard' fact* (statistic, quote, name/date, etc.) to support this point.
Technical details	
T1	Do not write your ideas as 'lists' or in bullet point form. Develop them in full and proper sentences.
T2	Write out in full the numbers one to nine (use numerals for 10 onwards).
T3	Write out the term/name in full the first time that you use it, with the abbreviation in brackets; thereafter you can use the abbreviation. For example: 'Irish Volunteer Force (IVF)' — thereafter you can just write 'IVF'.
Conclusion	
C1	See the comments I1 and I2 for the introduction above.
C2	You have too much information here; reduce this down to a *summary* of your main ideas.
C3	This is new information; it goes in the main body, not here.
C4	*Do not put your personal view* — just summarise the points that you have made in the main body.

ISBN: 9780170352581

Answers

Activity 2, pp. 6–7

1–14 are all primary; 15 is secondary.

Activity 1, p. 10

Required format is: Author's surname, author's initial(s). *Book title* (underlined if handwritten, *italics if typed*), publisher, city of publication, date of publication, page number(s).

1 McKinnon, M. *Independence in Foreign Policy*, Auckland University Press, Auckland, 1986, [page numbers?]
2 Simpson, T. *The Sugarbag Years*, [publisher?], Auckland, 1976, pp. 12–13
3 Hamish, K. *Book of Events*, Penguin, Wellington, [date of publication?], p. 45
4 Walker, R. *Struggle Without End*, Penguin, Christchurch, 1989, [page numbers?]
5 Scrimgeour, G. *The Scrim-Lee Papers*, Heinemann, Auckland, 1999, [page numbers?]
6 Spencer, W, [book title?], [publisher?], Christchurch, 1990, p. 39
7 Corbett, L. *Multi-Purpose Premium*, Otago University Press, Dunedin, 1992, p. 12 [perfect!]
8 Jason, M. *New Zealand Wars*, Pearson, Hamilton, 1992, p. 23

Activity 1, p. 14

The Contents page of a book contains main chapter headings. This is the best place to look for a 'big picture' overview. At the back of a book you'll find the Index. Look here for key words from your topic. The more pages on which your key words appear, the more information there will likely be on your topic. Once you start searching for information on the actual pages, quickly scan any headings. They will give you a stronger indication of what the information on the page is likely to be. In a big page of text where there are no headings, you can quickly scan the topic sentences to find out what is the main idea being covered in the whole paragraph. You can then decide to read the rest of the paragraph or move on to the next topic sentence!

Activity 2, pp. 14–15

A – The ways in which a revolution brings about significant change in a society. Yes, as expected.
B – The ways in which the Russian Revolution was significant globally in the 20th century. Yes, as expected (although it is brief).
C – The Russian Revolution's impact on WWI and WWII. Yes, as expected (although the impact on WWII was briefer than for WWI).
D – The Russian Revolution's impact on the last half of the 20th century. Yes, as expected.

Activity 3, p. 16

NOTE – your answers could differ from those given here; if so, check with your teacher. You will note that in many cases dates have not been underlined; this is because the events themselves are very specific.

a What were the main effects of the 'Great Depression' in 1930s New Zealand?
b What contribution did New Zealand women make at home to the war effort during 'World War Two'?
c Why did French agents bomb the '*Rainbow Warrior*' in Auckland harbour in 1985?
d What policies in 'South Africa' caused opposition to the '1981 Springbok Tour' to New Zealand?
e What actions did the 'Polynesian Panthers' take during the 1970s to help Pasifika people in Auckland?

Activity 4, p. 17

1	Reading age: 12–13	Percent of complex words: 20%
2	Reading age: 12–13	Percent of complex words: 12%
3	Reading age: 15–16	Percent of complex words: 17%
4	Reading age: 14–15	Percent of complex words: 23%

Activity 5, p. 18

Climate change: 5 (3)
Hitler: 4
United Nations: 41
Vietnam: 38
Suffrage: 18

Climate change: Greenhouse gases mostly from burning fossil fuels cause global warming
Hitler: The 'Hitler Youth' was his attempt to control and indoctrinate the youth.
United Nations: The Security Council is the part of the UN that tries to keep peace.
Vietnam War: The ARVN was the 'Army of the Republic of Vietnam' — the southern army.
Suffrage: New Zealand was the first to grant women the vote; Maori also got the vote early.

Activity 1, pp. 23–24

NOTE: you may find different information than what is shown below, but the conclusion you draw about 'source reliability' should be the same or similar.

1 Belich, J. *Making Peoples* (Penguin)
Education/position? (most recent): In 2011 Belich was appointed Beit Professor of Commonwealth History at Oxford University (England)
Other publications? (most recent): *Replenishing the Earth: The Settler Revolution and the Rise of the Anglo-world, 1783–1939*
Publisher information: Founded in Britain in 1935, it is now one of the 'Big 5' publishing houses.

2 Coney, S. *Standing in the Sunshine* (Viking)
Education/position? (most recent): She is a 'local body politician, writer, feminist, historian, and women's health campaigner.
Other publications? (most recent): *Under 'Writing Career' on Wikipedia it says that 'Coney is the author of more than 30 books on topics including history, feminism, and women's healthcare.'*

ISBN: 9780170352581

Publisher information: Viking Press is an American publishing company now owned by Penguin Random House. It was founded in 1925.

3 Pugsley, C. *The ANZAC Experience* (Reed Publishing)
Education/position? (most recent): Former army officer turned military historian; until 2014 he was Senior Lecturer in War Studies at the Royal Military Academy Sandhurst
Other publications? (most recent): *Sandhurst: A Tradition of Leadership*
Publisher information: Reed is one of NZ's oldest publishers, founded in 1907 and publishes over 100 titles a year.

4 Daley, C. *Beauty Queens and Physique Kings* (Auckland University Press)
Education/position? (most recent): Associate Professor of History and Dean of Graduate Studies at University of Auckland
Other publications? (most recent): *Beauty Queens and Physique Kings*
Publisher information: AUP is a leading NZ publisher founded in 1966 and an independent publisher based within The University of Auckland.

5 Harris, A. *Forty Years of Maori Protest* (Huia)
Education/position? (most recent): Senior Lecturer, History, University of Auckland.
Other publications? (most recent): *Tangata Whenua: An Illustrated History*
Publisher information: For over 20 years, Huia Publishers has been committed to producing quality books, describing the diverse range of Maori perspectives.

Summary

1 James Belich has been teaching university for a long time and has written many History books. Penguin is a huge company and has been around quite some time. Based on this brief information about Belich and Penguin this source is reliable.

2 Although Coney is not an historian by training she has written a lot of academic-level books which suggests that she would use the same skills as an historian. Viking Press has been around a long time as is now owned by Penguin. Based on this brief information about Coney and Penguin this source is reliable.

3 Pugsley is a military historian who started out in the military. As a Senior Lecturer in War Studies he will have a lot of experience and (presumably) academic training. Reed Publishers is a New Zealand publisher that has been around for a long time. Based on this brief information about Pugsley and Reed this source is reliable.

4 Daley is an historian at the University of Auckland and has a high position in the department. AUP is the University's own publishing company so it will publish only quality works. Based on this brief information about Daley and AUP this source is reliable.

5 Aroha Harris also has a senior position in the History department at the University of Auckland. Huia Publishers specialise in publishing Maori perspectives and has been doing so for 20 years. Although it is more specialist than the other publishers here it still has a good reputation. Based on this brief information about Harris and Huia this source is reliable.

Activity 2, p. 27

The cartoonist is making the point that while bloggers are an unreliable source of information so too can be news outlets (especially ones like Fox network that usually take a pro-Republican point of view).

Activity 3, pp. 29–31

Website 1

1 **Generally reliable?** No

2 **Explanation of your decision:** While it looks like the creators of this site mean well, there is nothing here on their qualifications. The focus also seems to be on young children and 'creativity' rather than reliable information.

3 **Short quote (as evidence):**
- We began by designing educational games for our own children
- Our company's mission is to produce educational materials that emphasize creativity and the pure enjoyment of learning.

Website 2

1 **Generally reliable?** Yes

2 **Explanation of your decision**: John Simkin has written lots of History books (probably aimed at school children) over a long period and has high level qualifications. He also writes for some reputable publications.

3 **Short quote (as evidence):**
- Over the last twenty years I have written over one dozen history books such as *Gandhi* (1987), *Hitler* (1988), *Making of the United Kingdom* (1992), and *The Medieval Village* (1996).
- I also produced online material for the *Electronic Telegraph*, the European Virtual School and the *Guardian* newspaper's educational website, *Learn*.

Website 3

1 **Generally reliable?** No / More information needed

2 **Explanation of your decision**: It's possible that the 'journalists' mentioned have the right qualifications and experience but we simply don't know. If this was all the information we had then it would have to be considered an unreliable site.

3 **Short quote (as evidence):**
- best collection of journalists

Website 4

1 **Generally reliable?** No / More information needed

2 **Explanation of your decision**: This might be all right if we can find out the qualifications and experience of the person who wrote the article we were interested in, but if this information isn't available then it would have to be considered unreliable.

3 **Short quote (as evidence):**
- war veterans
- librarians, lawyers
- You can contribute, too, if you have the right experience and a desire to spread knowledge to other people.

Website 5

1 **Generally reliable?** Yes

2 **Explanation of your decision**: Although Simkin is not an historian he has been university trained and has had a long career as a (very good, apparently) History teacher. More importantly, he has written a large number of history textbooks (for schools) so presumably he knows his history.

3 **Short quote (as evidence):**
- studied Modern history at Oxford University, and graduated in 1974.
- Head of History in 1979 at Greenfield School
- described in the education magazine *Teaching History* as 'the best teacher out there'.
- author of more than 70 history textbooks

Activities 1–5, pp. 36–42

NOTE: Your responses may well be different. If so, check with your teacher.

Activity 1

1 Lydia Hotchkiss, writing to her children who are (presumably) in the South. A guess would be that she is a white American.

2 It was written December 8th, 1859 when it seems there was slavery in the South and the possibility of war.

3 Lydia Hotchkiss is in Windsor, Augusta County, Virginia, which is in the North of the USA. It reads like a letter written from her home, which appears to be a small village.

4 It's a personal letter that seems to be to let her children know what's been going on in the village, but also to let them know (perhaps to reassure them) that she at least does not care about the issues of slavery (if the Southerners believe that God approves) and that she thinks there won't be war.

5 Other similar letters from different northerners (and southerners) to see what they think about the issue of slavery, plus other letters by Lydia Hotchkiss to see if her view changed over time. Newspaper reports would also give us a wider view on the issues of slavery/war. Some slave letters, if such things exist, would be good so that we can hear their side of the story.

6 Judging by the spelling mistakes, Lydia Hotchkiss has had only a certain level of schooling, but with the very personal nature of the letter it does show that it is her actually writing it.

Strengths of the source

It is a personal letter so we can hear the voice of a northerner at this time of trouble that is presumably being honest about her views, although she may also be trying to reassure her children that there is no danger. Because it is not written by someone who is extremely well educated we are hearing from an 'ordinary' American. It is a female perspective.

Any weaknesses/limitations of the source

This is Lydia Hotchkiss's view at this point in time only (it might change later or already have changed), and it is the view of only one person. It is hard to know if from her village she had a wider understanding of the issues going on at this time.

Overall comment on reliability of this source in terms of the events described.

This is a very valuable and reliable source for the historian studying this time period in the United States. Its strengths make it useful for hearing a certain perspective and its limitations can be overcome by finding more sources from a variety of people/groups.

Activity 2

1 It is an address/speech from a meeting 'of Negroes' and the person who wrote it was presumably either a spokesperson or part of some sort of committee form the meeting.

2 August 5th, 1865. The US Civil War is over and the slaves have been freed, but it seems that conditions for blacks have not much improved.

3 At the three-day meeting held in Alexandria, Virginia.

4 The address is being sent to the 'Loyal Citizens and US Congress'. Its purpose is most likely to inform the US people and Congress that things are not satisfactory for black people, with many of the 'enemies' of the black people set free already. The address also calls for the right of blacks to vote so they can look out for themselves.

5 Most interesting would be find out what was Congress's reaction to this address in the official record. Maybe there were newspaper reports, too. It would also be good to know if blacks elsewhere in the US felt the same — were there similar meetings held in other places? How did the 'enemies' of the black people feel about the situation at the time? There might be letters or even a record in the archives of the pardons they were given.

6 As noted above, it looks like it was the product of a committee, so it would be interesting to know how long it took, were there many changes made or arguments over the wording? It also suggests that at least some black people could read and write.

Strengths of the source

As a clear expression of at least how some black people felt about the situation after the civil war and what they wanted to make things better (the vote), this is excellent. It represents more than just one person's opinion and suggests that the situation must have been concerning enough for black people to meet. As it went to Congress there might well be some record of how Congress responded. Presumably one or more of the blacks in attendance wrote.

Any weaknesses/limitations of the source

We don't know how many black people attended the meeting, or how representative this meeting was of the views of blacks elsewhere. We don't have a lot of information on *exactly* what concerns the blacks had.

Overall comment on reliability of this source in terms of the events described.

This is an excellent source, as noted, and its limitations could mostly be dealt with by finding additional sources and viewpoints.

Activity 3

1 A member of the Abbey of Xanten, as it finishes by saying 'This finishes my report …' Perhaps the person is the record-keeper for the Abbey.

2 It says the year is 845 ('the Year of our Lord eight hundred and forty-five'), a year in which there has been two earthquakes and an invasion by Vikings.

3 It seems like he must be at the Abbey, although he does also seem to know about other things that are going on beyond it, so either he travels around or news of the rest of the country comes through to the Abbey.

4 It looks like it is an ongoing record for the Abbey, like an official diary. The fact that the writer knows other things going on might mean that such records are shared, perhaps with other abbeys.

5 Any further existing records from this abbey, as well as from any others. This report is critical of the King (Charles), so it would be good to hear his point of view. Perhaps one day the Christian slaves were released; if so, their accounts would be very interesting, as would the Vikings own accounts, if they left any.

6 Obviously this member of the Abbey could write (unless he dictated it to someone who could). Perhaps it was in some sort of journal/diary, which might explain why this record survived.

Strengths of the source

If this is an official account of the Abbey then it is very reliable and useful. Presumably the account is meant for the Abbey alone, which would make it very honest.

Any weaknesses/limitations of the source

If the report was meant for sending to a superior somewhere then it might be a little bit less reliable, as the Abbey might want to 'paint a good picture' of itself, although there is actually nothing much here about Xanten Abbey itself. It is a viewpoint only from someone who can read and write, so there might be other views to try to find.

Overall comment on reliability of this source in terms of the events described.

This is another excellent source, as noted, and its limitations could also mostly be dealt with by finding additional sources and viewpoints.

Activity 4

1 Someone who, as a young German girl at the end of WWII, lived through the trouble in Berlin between the Russians and America/Britain.

2 It seems to have been created in more recent times ('I may be old and nearly at the end of my life …') but is remembering some sort of post-war crisis in Berlin that saw Stalin blockade West Berlin.

3 The source itself seems to have been created during something like a visit to a school or some other similar event, but she was actually living in Berlin itself during the events described.

4 It seems to be a speech or similar to share the speaker's experiences with young people of what life was like during the crisis and how the Americans/British 'risked their lives for us' even though they had been enemies a few years before. The speaker seems to want to encourage the young people to think well of the British and Americans ('You young people today forget what the Americans and British did for us').

5 Other stories of those who also lived through the crisis, the views of the American/British pilots who risked their lives, and the Soviet view — why did they blockade West Berlin? Newspaper reports from both sides, and any speeches by the leaders of the three countries involved would also be good.

6 It's either the written version of the speaker's talk to the 'young people' or someone recorded it and wrote it down.

Strengths of the source

This is quite reliable for telling us what life was like during the crisis from someone who actually lived through it as the speaker was there. There is some good detail even though it is many years later.

Any weaknesses/limitations of the source

It is clearly many years later and the speaker seems to be older or even elderly; their memory may not be the best. The speaker is also favourable towards the Americans/British so *might* have presented what they did in a more positive light. We don't know the circumstances behind the giving of the speech to the young audience; was it to encourage positive feelings in the youth towards America/Britain? Does the speaker now work for the government of one of these countries?

Overall comment on reliability of this source in terms of the events described.

This is a very good source but it would be important to find records from the actual time to check that this speaker has remembered things correctly, or is not unduly biased towards the British/Americans.

Activity 5

1 A man called Phillip Johnston who lives in California (USA). He seems quite well informed about events, so probably keeps up with the news. He clearly is not at all awed by writing to the President — 'you were just too dumb …' and 'even your feeble mind …' and it seems that he feels quite within his rights to give the President a piece of his mind!

2 September 12, 1948; the 'Berlin Crisis' in the last source is happening.

 ISBN: 9780170352581

3 He's presumably at his home in California, a long way away from the events.
4 He is very worried that the President – through what he says as poor policy and stupidity – will drag America into another war (it is only three years after the end of WWII). He wants to influence the President in terms of his dealings with Russia to seek a peaceful solution. Or, at the least, it is to let the President know how disgusted he is with his policies.
5 Did the President reply?! What was in the article from the *Los Angeles Times* of September 12? Did the President receive other similar letters? Any opinion polls taken at this time to see how Americans generally felt about the President's handling of the Crisis would be useful.
6 This seems to be a straightforward letter from a US citizen to the President. It is interesting that it was kept in the archives.

Strengths of the source

It is very reliable as a clear opinion of at least one citizen with regards to the Berlin Crisis. The writer clearly has some knowledge of events.

Any weaknesses/limitations of the source

It is only one letter, quite rudely written, so it might be a minority view. More sources are needed. While it is reliable for telling us how this citizen felt, it might not be so reliable in terms of the actual details/background of the Crisis, or the President's handling of it.

Overall comment on reliability of this source in terms of the events described.

As noted, this is a very reliable and useful source for telling us how this one person feels about the Berlin Crisis and the President's handling of it. It also reveals that this person wasn't fearful that his strong views would get him in trouble. It's not necessarily as reliable for telling us how well (or not) the President did handle this crisis.

Activities 6–11, pp. 48–56

NOTE: your responses may be different to those given here. If so, check with your teacher.

Activity 6, Image 1

1 Maybe a journalist or someone recording the march for the protesters.
2 The date is 1963 and the protest seems to be about jobs and equal rights. Most of the marchers are black (one looks like Martin Luther King) so it could be a black civil rights protest. It's in Washington, the US capital.
3 The photographer is in front of the marchers, perhaps walking backwards taking photos while the crowd moves forward. The photographer would be clearly seen by the crowd so they'd know he/she was there, but they don't seem to mind.
4 Maybe for a newspaper or similar, to show how well attended the protest was and maybe even to show that there are some white people there, too. This is to inform the wider American public.
5 Police photographs/reports; other journalists' photographs; newspaper reports; copies of any speeches made. It would be good, too, to hear from women and white marchers — as well as opponents' views on the march.
6 This doesn't appear to be posed in any way and is a 'live action' shot. Perhaps it is taken in such a way as to emphasise the size of the crowd and a sample of the sorts of people in it? The people don't seem to mind the camera being there.

Usefulness of the source

This is very useful for showing us that the marchers *can* march without harassment from the police (none in sight). The protesters are mostly black men (there are some women and even a few whites, at least in this image), but there don't appear to be many young people. All are well dressed and they appear to be non-violent. The cause of the march, according to the signs, is for jobs and equal rights. Some signs call for the end of segregation in schools. It is the sort of image that might appear in a newspaper of the time to inform Americans about this event. It appears to be a 'natural' shot telling us how things really were.

Any weaknesses/limitations of the source

It is just one photograph, so we'd need more information to find out how widespread/large the march was, and if it was all as peaceful as this. The angle is quite low so we can't see how big this crowd is.

Activity 7, Image 2

1 This could be the work of a war photographer or perhaps one of the troops, but there might not be time for a solider to take this as it looks like the battle is happening.
2 1917, so it is very likely during WWI.
3 In the trenches right amongst the battle.
4 If they were a war journalist then there job is to take photos to record the conflict. These could be for the use of military planners or for publishing in newspapers (given that it is wartime, such a photo could possibly be used for propaganda, although it doesn't look particularly 'heroic').
5 Other photos from here and other parts of the Western Front. Images from when it has been raining (to see what conditions are lie then); military reports; newspapers to see if the photo appeared and, if so, what story went with it. Letters and diaries of the men involved.
6 This photographer is right amongst the conflict; nothing appears to be 'posed' so it's a 'live action' shot. It's quite clear (no blurring) so either the technology has improved by this time or there's not much movement.

Usefulness of the source

Because does not appear to be posed it gives us a good idea of what the battlefield was like (churned up) and thus fighting conditions. The trenches are clearly shown, although they might have been shelled heavily as they're not very deep.

Any weaknesses/limitations of the source

It's hard to tell if the two soldiers in the distance are on the other side and are attacking the trenches, or not. This image only provides a very narrow idea of the war's conditions, in this one area at this one time. We can't actually see a lot. Are these the only soldiers in this sector? We definitely need more information/sources.

Activity 8, Image 3

1 A newspaper photographer or a member of the suffrage campaign?
2 The date on the sign says that there is going to be a vote (presumably on the suffrage issue) on September 3, 1912, so this is likely to have been taken just prior to that. The style of clothing looks 'old'. The issue, as noted, is the right of women to vote which they clearly don't have, at least in Ohio.
3 The photographer appears to have been just across the street. It doesn't seem to be a busy street as no one else is in the image.
4 Probably as part of a newspaper report on the suffrage campaign, so to inform the public. The image doesn't seem to be trying to look particularly positive *or* negative towards the suffrage goal. It could also be by the suffrage campaigners themselves, to keep a record and perhaps to share with other campaigners.
5 Newspaper reports on the campaign, both in Ohio and elsewhere. The outcome of the vote on Septebmer 3, 1912. Diary entries/letters of the suffrage campaigners. Views of those opposed to suffrage.
6 It looks natural as some people are looking at the camera (aware of it) but others are not. The people don't seem to mind the camera being there. Either the technology is better or the people are all standing fairly still as there is no blurring

Usefulness of the source

It is very useful for telling us that women did not have the vote in 1912 (at least in Ohio) but that at least some were active in campaigning for it. They have an office, so are quite organised and there must be some funding to pay for it. The sign is appealing to *men* to learn about and vote for women's suffrage; this makes sense as only men can vote. There is one - and perhaps a second - man, so it is not women campaigning entirely on their own. Everything is peaceful so it doesn't look like there is a strong negative reaction to the campaign, at least not in this photo. All the people are white and well-dressed, and not 'youth'.

Any weaknesses/limitations of the source

As always with a single source, we can't tell too much from this one image. It doesn't look like there is much happening so perhaps it is before an event of some sort.

Activity 9, Image 4

1 A newspaper (or freelance) photographer, or a member of the protest group, or possibly even the police.
2 1981. It is a protest march against 'the Tour' *[Springbok Tour]* and the marchers also are against apartheid *[the segregationist policy in South Africa]*. It's at night-time, or at least early evening, perhaps so that more people can be part of it.
3 The shot is from higher up above the crowd, presumably in order to get a good view, so the photographer might be on top of a building or in a second-storey window.

4 This could be for a newspaper, in which case it would be to inform the public. If it was one of the protesters themselves taking the photograph, then it would be to keep a record and perhaps to study afterwards in terms of strategy and/or to ensure any police violence (if there was any) was captured on film. If the police took it, it could be to help identify protesters later and/or to use as evidence if there was any trouble.
5 Newspaper and police reports would be useful. Perspectives from protesters (diaries, interviews, letters), as well as the impact such protests had on the players (from both sides). Also whether or not such protests had any impact on apartheid. We could investigate and find out more about the groups whose names are on some of the banners. We could also look at other protests elsewhere in NZ — were they similar?
6 The photographer has positioned him/her-self to get a good shot down the length of the street where the protest is occurring. It's a 'live action' photo so there is no staging. It's hard to tell but few, if any, people are looking at the camera so they may not be aware of its presence. The picture is black and white even though it is 1981 [this might be because newspapers only printed in black and white then].

Usefulness of the source

This gives us a very good idea of what an anti-Tour protest march looked like. We can see the banners, some of which identify the groups involved; some are 'home-made' and some appear to be printed off ('mass produced'). We can get an idea of how many people turned out, at least to this one in Dunedin. There seems to be a mix of men and women of all ages (no children?), and most look to be Pakeha. There are some police but they do not appear to be concerned by the crowd, presumably because it is peaceful. Cars are still parked on the side of the road, suggesting that the public didn't expect any violence or trouble.

Any weaknesses/limitations of the source

As always, more than just this one source is required in order to make any firm generalisations about anti-Tour protests, even this one in Dunedin. Perhaps it turned violent later, whether due to police or protester actions ...

Activity 10, Image 5

1 A newspaper photographer or interested resident (who owns a camera) or even the town photographer. It is 1878 so there probably aren't that many people with cameras.
2 1878, during a flood in Queenstown. There is some snow on the mountains but not a lot, so maybe spring or autumn? The style of the buildings and the clothing the people are wearing all look 'old', too.
3 The photograph is taken from the street looking towards the lake where flood waters have risen up.
4 If the image was taken by a newspaper photographer then it would be to publish and inform the public. If it was taken by a private person then it might be to just keep a personal record of this flood. Possibly it's even for insurance purposes ...?
5 There would probably be newspaper (and maybe police) reports of the flood, and perhaps some letters or diary entries from people affected. If there were insurance claims then there might be records of those, too.
6 It's hard to tell but it looks as though everyone is looking at the camera. They are motionless enough for those in the image not to have blurred. Perhaps the photographer asked everyone to be still and look their way. However, the flood is not in any way 'posed' so the event is realistic.

Usefulness of the source

This image gives us a good idea of what one Queenstown waterfront street looked like (the road is not paved, for example, and there are no vehicles of any sort). One side of the street appears to have more prosperous stone buildings while the other has less prosperous looking wooden ones. It also shows us a potential threat to Queenstown: flooding — there is a rowboat of some sort on the floodwaters! The vessel on the lake shows us that steam technology was in use. There are no telephone or telegraph lines — too early? Nor are there any streetlights; it must have been tricky to walk around at night. All the bystanders seem to be men. Perhaps women's clothing at this time didn't let them come out for a look?

Any weaknesses/limitations of the source

As with any single image, we cannot draw too many conclusions without further sources. Perhaps the flooding was bad only in this place. We don't get much of an idea of how big Queenstown was at this time.

Activity 11, Image 6

1 Presumably a military photographer.
2 May 1915. The caption tells us that the troops are (presumably) on their way to land at Gallipoli, during WWI. It's daytime on a reasonably fine and calm day (the sea is not rough). In the northern hemisphere it's springtime.
3 Hard to know! The photographer might be up on a wheelhouse (tall structure where the boat is steered from) or possibly up some sort of mast. Either that or he's on a bigger vessel that is very close to this one. It is even possible that the photographer is on a jetty/wharf and that this is actually close to land ...
4 If they were a military photographer then it would be at least to keep a record of events. The image *might* be used as 'propaganda' if the military/government thought it was useful enough, in order to create a positive image of the war. In this case it *could* end up on recruiting posters or in newspapers to persuade people to support the war effort.
5 Other such photographs, particularly once the boat landed and off-loaded the troops. Official military records; private letters and diaries of the soldiers telling of their experiences.
6 A number of the troops are looking at the camera, so they know it is there. It's not a 'staged' photo as such, because the men are (presumably) off to join the fight. It's hard to tell, but some/many are 'smiling for the camera'. There's no blurring, even though there must be movement due to the sea, so perhaps the film technology is quite good by now.

Usefulness of the source

This image gives us a good idea of the conditions for the soldiers being transported (presumably) to the fight. (There don't appear to be any wounded men so they're probably not coming back.) They are densely packed in and would presumably suffer a lot of casualties if they came under enemy fire. These are likely to be Allied troops (i.e. New Zealand, Australian, British and/or French — all appear to be 'whites'). We can see some evidence of the nature of their uniforms/helmets and the gear each carried, although more *might* be stowed elsewhere on the boat.

Any weaknesses/limitations of the source

As for all of the other sources here, one image is not sufficient to draw strong conclusions. We do not know exactly which country these men are from or if they are actually going off to battle (it *could* be a training exercise). It's hard to tell the ages of the men, so we'd need to get information from elsewhere to make some generalisations about that aspect.

Activity 13, pp. 61–62

1	Struggle	2	Freedom
3	Trouble	4	Oppression
5	War	6	Overcoming difficulties or obstacles
7	Good idea	8	Victory

Activity 14, pp. 66–72

NOTE: Your responses may well be different. If so, check with your teacher.

Cartoon A

1 'Modern times' – 2013. The issue is the way that technology has become such a big part of our lives.
2 In the first frame the phone owner is bigger/dominant and is making demands of the phone, but in the second frame he is smaller and bowing down to the much larger phone that is making demands of him.
3 The cartoonist is trying to show the difference between how we believe technology should be part of our lives and how it actually is in reality.
4 This is a reasonably straightforward cartoon where colour, shading, drawing style and symbols aren't really used to communicate ideas, but the dialogue between the owner and the phone, plus the 'In your mind' and 'In reality' captions, show how the owner has unexpectedly become the slave of the phone!
5 Instead of being a 'servant' to us and making our lives easier these new phones have demanded more of our time and attention, making us slaves to them!

Cartoon B

1 1985. Hospital waiting times is the issue.
2 The doctor and 'patient'.
3 The patient has died and become a skeleton due to being so long on the waiting list. The skeleton image exaggerates the wait but makes the point.

ISBN: 9780170352581

4 We can see the sign 'Admissions' that signals it's a hospital, and the 'Waiting List' heading is obvious for us to see; this helps us understand why the patient has become a skeleton. The exaggeration here is in the waiting time *[although some people do in fact die while on the waiting list]*. The skeleton is the only symbol, of waiting an overly long time.
5 Hospital waiting lists are too long and people are being affected by it (dying even). It might well be a criticism of government policies that mean hospitals don't have enough resources to see patients quickly.

Cartoon C

1 1984. There seems to be some issue about crime and unemployment.
2 Both the person labelled 'Crime' and the one labelled 'Unemployment' are equal sized/prominent, perhaps to show that they are equal in importance. There are no other characters.
3 Perhaps it is easier to draw 'Crime' and 'Unemployment' as people. They are running away together, hand-in-hand, meaning that they have a close relationship.
4 The dialogue backs up the image by saying that the two issues are linked, but politicians only focus on one — crime. The drawing style is rather basic bus doesn't seem to be making any particular point in itself. The two people are actually symbols that represent the problems of 'crime' and 'unemployment'.
5 As mentioned above, politicians seem to target 'Crime' alone to 'beat' as though it has no link to unemployment. This cartoonist seems to believe that there is, in fact, a link between the two issues. Perhaps Bromhead is criticising the government for focusing on one but not the other.

Cartoon D

1 It is set in 1962 and there seems to be some sort of struggle going on between the leaders of Russia and America.
2 Both leaders appear to be shown equally, suggesting that each is as powerful or important as the other. Both are well-dressed. There are no other characters.
3 The arm-wrestle shows that there is a struggle that one or the other could win. However, both have their fingers poised above a button which it seems will detonate the bomb under the other person if pressed.
4 The sweat and look on Khrushchev's face might suggest that he is losing the struggle; Kennedy perhaps seems more determined and in control. The 'struggle lines' around their clenched hands show that there is indeed a struggle going on. There doesn't seem to be any caricature or use of bold lines. The bombs would be a symbol for destruction.
5 It looks as though even if one side wins the arm wrestle then the other can push their button and destroy their opponent. Either one can do this so, in a way, neither can without risking their own lives (and their country?).

Cartoon E

1 It looks like a meeting about climate change in relatively recent times (2013). The audience appears to be ethnically mixed, so it *could* be a global meeting?
2 The two most important characters are the man speaking on stage and the other man from the audience questioning him. The rest of the audience don't play much of a part.
3 The man on stage is in a suit and the audience man is in a shirt and tie; they both seem 'respectable', as do what we can see of the rest of the audience.
4 The presentation on stage shows a list of what could be outcomes of taking action, but the man in the audience does not seem to be on board with this view — he thinks it might be all a hoax. There doesn't seem to be any caricature, nor is colour/shading/drawing style particularly relevant.
5 The man on stage is pointing out the (beneficial) outcomes of taking action on climate change, but the man from the audience isn't convinced that there is a need to take action. The cartoonist's point is that even if somehow it (climate change) was a hoax (or wrong), the changes would still be good to make anyway.

Cartoon F

1 The cartoon is from 2014, and appears to be something about an 'exit strategy' from Iraq.
2 None of the three characters appear to be any more prominent than the others, although one does look like 'Uncle Sam'/America. The other two might represent countries, as well?
3 They are going around and around on an endless 'staircase' that has no endpoint. This suggests that (with the caption explanation of what an 'exit strategy' is) there is no obvious way off the staircase.
4 Shading and drawing style don't seem to be particularly significant here, and the 'Uncle Sam' figure suggests that America is involved. Some of the signage around the endless staircase backs up the point of no exit ('No exit', 'Back to square one') but without additional information the meaning of the other signs is unclear.
5 It looks like America and perhaps some other countries have got themselves into a situation, most likely in Iraq, that they didn't make any plans for in terms of how to get out again, and now they can't. Judging by the pointlessness of going round and round the staircase, the cartoonist probably thinks this has been a bad idea.

Activity 15, p. 73

NOTE: if you have a different response and are not sure about it, ask your teacher.

1 OPINION
2 OPINION (unless weather statistics were provided to prove otherwise)
3 OPINION (unless, e.g., opinion poll statistics were provided to prove otherwise)
4 FACT (rising petrol prices affect more than just those who drive cars)
5 FACT (assuming that these are accurate statistics)
6 FACT (assuming that the protester's own personal *opinion* has been accurately reported)
7 FACT (first part) and OPINION (second part, unless the onlookers all *said they were relieved)*
8 FACT (first part) and OPINION (second part, unless the jury *said they had no problems* coming up with a guilty verdict)
9 OPINION (first part, unless the judge *said she was grumpy*) and FACT (second part,)
10 FACT

Activity 16, p. 75

NOTE: you may not agree with all of these answers; if so, discuss them with the class.

1 FACT (first part) and OPINION (second part; there could be other reasons why the officer *appeared* unfit)
2 FACT
3 OPINION — 'sneaked' and 'determined' especially (perhaps even 'pursued' is an opinion)
4 OPINION — 'guilty-looking', FACT (second part)
5 FACT (unless 'ran' is considered an opinion …)
6 OPINION — 'frightened', FACT (second part)
7 OPINION — 'well-dressed' and 'tore down', FACT (second part; presumably the sweat was obvious …)
8 FACT (first part; 'sprinting' does suggest very fast running) and OPINION (second part; the officer might have been worried, concerned etc rather than angry.)

Activity 1, p. 80–6 *see page 140*

Activity 1, p. 91

1 At a rally in 1939, Hitler announced: 'We've entered a new era, and the people's self-belief will be put to the test.'
2 According to Prime Minister Lange, New Zealand's anti-nuclear law proved its worth when it was most needed.
3 It's been a long time since they've visited the battle site.
4 The woman's hat nearly blew off its owner's head!
5 The women's suffrage movement was finally successful in winning the vote in 1893.
6 'Well, that's about it,' she said, although they weren't actually finished with their apostrophe tasks.
7 'It isn't fair; we can't be expected to do the whole class's work ourselves,' said those who had finished their activities quickly.
8 'Practice makes perfect,' the teacher said as she took the boys' work in but let the girls continue, as they'd had less time.

Activity 1, pp. 80–84

1 **Focus question**: 'How did the government respond to the different forms of Maori leadership?'

Faced with a Pakeha government that neglected their concerns, Maori leaders had three main choices. Some became part of the Pakeha system. They did this by being elected to Parliament in one of the four Maori seats. From there they worked inside the Pakeha government to try to change things. However, with only four Maori members they did not have much influence over the government. A second option, taken up eventually by some traditional tribal leaders, was to work alongside the Pakeha system. At first, governments paid little attention to these tribal leaders. Soon, however, officials came to realise that they provided an effective link to Maori communities. A third option, taken up by one notable Maori leader in the 20th century, was to build a separate community, outside direct Pakeha influence. The government did not like separatist movements and, as with earlier cases, responded with armed force.

> Neglect of Maori concerns by the government …
>
> … because Maori had only four MPs in Parliament.
>
> There was some change and officials at least began to see Maori leaders as a link to their communities.
>
> 'Separatist' Maori leaders were not tolerated.

2 **Focus question**: 'What social changes occurred in the 1920s in many countries?'

In the 1920s, there was a reaction amongst the public to the gloom of World War One and the hardship it represented. This period, lasting until the Great Depression began in 1929, has become known as the 'Jazz Age' or the 'Roaring Twenties'. Jazz music came from African-American origins, but was adapted to be acceptable to a white American audience. The newly developed commercial radio stations helped spread it, and its popularity grew. With it came new dance crazes such as the Charleston. Young people in the 1920s were very much influenced by jazz, and it became the 'sound track' of a rebellion against the traditional culture of previous generations.

From America, the music and its associated culture spread across the Atlantic to Europe (and, eventually, to New Zealand too). In America, those who embraced the new ways were known as 'flappers', and in Britain as 'Bright Young People'. Well-to-do women adopted daring new fashions such as short skirts, make-up and bobbed haircuts. They took up drinking and smoking in public, began wearing make-up, and went out unchaperoned *[without an older woman as escort]*. The money flowing due to the Dawes Plan helped create a wider sense of prosperity. The bad times, it seemed, were over.

> People wanted more 'fun' after the gloom of WWI.
>
> New jazz music spread in America and with it new dance crazes, the 'sound-track of rebellion' for young people.
>
> New sub-cultures developed. Well-off women adopted new daring fashions and smoked and drank in public.

3 **Focus question**: 'How did governments in different countries deal with the problems of the Great Depression, 1929–35?'

Sweden was one of the few countries where the people survived the Depression relatively unscathed *[unharmed]*. Sweden already had a history of providing social welfare for its people, dating back to 1914. By 1925, all schoolchildren were being provided with a free daily meal. In 1931, the Social Democratic Party won the election in a landslide *[sweeping]* victory. The new government provided unemployment benefits, family allowances and old-age pensions, as well as supporting sickness funds. Sweden rejected the view held in the US and other countries such as New Zealand at this time, that poverty was the fault of the individual. In these countries, government support for the people was minimal. However, when the first Labour government was elected in New Zealand in 1935, it followed policies similar to Sweden's.

In Japan, the military became more influential due to the Depression. Japan had industrialised *[built factories]* rapidly after WWI, and was badly affected in the early 1930s when other countries cut back their imports of Japanese products. Nearly 50 percent of Japan's heavy industry closed, and the vital silk export trade was destroyed. However, Japan's main problem was different to that of most countries. Japan lacked the raw materials it needed for its factories, and these had to be bought from overseas.

During the 1920s, Japan had imported iron, rubber and oil to maintain its strong economic growth. Most of these resources came from the United States. In the 1930s, Japan lacked the money to buy them. Elements within the Japanese government, and nationalists [strongly patriotic people] outside it, felt that an alternative would be to simply take over resource-rich territories.

> In Sweden the government provided various benefits to help people; it did not blame people for their poverty as in NZ and the US, where support was limited. In NZ the newly elected Labour government introduced policies like Sweden's.
>
> In Japan the military grew more powerful.
>
> Some government members looked to simply taking the needed resources.

4 **Focus question**: 'What actions were taken by the government in an attempt to maintain the British nature of "New Zealand identity"?'

As the war clouds again gathered in Europe in the late 1930s, most Pakeha New Zealanders still felt that they were British. Many Maori also felt part of the British Empire, to greater or lesser degrees. The experiences of WWI made many New Zealanders feel not so much that they had developed a separate identity, but that they had proved themselves to be 'better British'. Smaller groups, such as the relatively few Chinese, Indians, Lebanese and Dalmatians in the country, did their best to be part of this identity. If not, they at least tried to be inconspicuous *[low key]* in terms of their own cultural values.

One of the 'threats' to New Zealand's sense of 'better British' identity came from American cultural influences. From the early 1920s, concern was being raised about the American presence in the media. In 1927, 350 out of the 400 films shown in New Zealand were from the United States. This led to the introduction of a law in 1928 for quotas of British films. By the 1930s, the proportion of British films being shown had increased to 50 percent.

When American radio serials began to be broadcast in the early 1930s, there was further criticism of them as 'un-British'. One critic noted that New Zealanders were imitating Americans by saying 'Okay, baby'. Apart from a brief period during WWII, American radio serials were banned until the 1960s. Australian radio serials were deemed *[considered]* to be more acceptable, and they became popular.

> Law passed by the government to ensure British films were shown in NZ, reinforcing 'Britishness'.
>
> Presumably this was another government ban on US radio programmes.

5 **Focus question**: 'What strategies did Keith Park use to protect England from attack?'

Keith Park was born in Thames, Coromandel. He was schooled at King's College in Auckland, as well as Otago Boys' High School in Dunedin. In WWI he fought at Gallipoli, and then at the Battle of the Somme. It was during this time that he came to appreciate the importance of aerial reconnaissance *['spying' from the air]* over enemy positions. In October 1916 he was blown off his horse by a German shell and his Army days were over. He decided to join the Royal Flying Corps. By the end of WWI, he had earned the Military Cross for shooting down a German aircraft and damaging three others. He also received the Distinguished Flying Cross and the French Croix de Guerre, among other awards. After the war he became a flight instructor. He steadily rose through the ranks to become a staff officer to Air Chief Marshal Hugh Dowding by 1938.

In April 1940, prior to the fall of France and the Battle of Britain, Air Vice Marshal Park was put in charge of defending the skies above London and southeast England. In this role, he organised fighter patrols over the French coast. He also co-ordinated fighter defences against German attacks during the Battle of Britain. He supported Dowding's plan to only deploy *[put into action]* a small number of fighters to resist each wave of the *Luftwaffe*. This was because the Royal Air Force simply did not have enough planes or pilots. To preserve this limited strength, Park ordered the pilots to focus on shooting down just the German bombers. It was these, and not the escorting fighters, that would cause the most damage. To inspire his men, as often as possible he flew his personal Hurricane fighter — the 'OK1' — to visit the airfields where the pilots were stationed.

After the war, Air Chief Marshal Sir Arthur Tedder (who was also Deputy Supreme Commander under General Dwight Eisenhower for the 'D-Day' invasion) noted that: *'If any one man won the Battle of Britain, [park] did. I do not believe it is realised how much that one man, with his leadership, his calm judgement and his skill, did to save, not only this country [Britain], but the world.'*

> Park was in charge of organising fighter defences, supporting the idea of sending up just small groups of fighters to meet the Germans.
>
> Park's strategy was to just focus on shooting down the bombers as they caused the most damage.
>
> He inspired his men by visiting the various airfields.
>
> Air Chief Marshal Sir Arthur Tedder said that Park used his 'leadership, his calm judgement and his skill' to save Britain — and the world!

6 **Focus question**: 'What impact did New Zealand women gaining the vote in 1893 have on government policies?'

> Nothing here is relevant!

Activity 1, p. 93

'Kete 1' label: Cars
'Kete 2' label: Vegetables
'Kete 3' label: Dogs
'Kete 4' label: Fruit

'Kete 1' label: Fast food outlets
'Kete 2' label: Music genres
'Kete 3' label: School subjects
'Kete 4' label: Film genres

ISBN: 9780170352581

Activity 2, p. 95

THE 1953–1954 ROYAL TOUR TO NEW ZEALAND

One of the clearest indications of how most New Zealanders felt about Britain was the 1953–1954 Royal Tour by the Queen. This was a major event for several reasons. Firstly, Pakeha New Zealanders — and a number of Maori — still identified closely with Britain and the Commonwealth. Several years earlier New Zealanders had still been dying as part of Britain's effort to defeat the enemy in the war. Also, most of New Zealand's import and export trade was with Britain. Furthermore, many of the country's immigrants at the time were from just one country. Finally, New Zealand in the 1950s was booming. Wartime restrictions were over, and a New Zealander had in conquered Mt Everest for the first time. [when?] The Royal Tour – the first by a reigning *[ruling]* monarch [what was her name?] — seemed to cap off a perfect year.

The Queen and her husband toured through many towns and attended a large number of different functions in five weeks. In some places sheep were dyed red, white and blue in displays of patriotism. In others, instructions were given on how to plant flower gardens in similar patriotic colours. Towns [which ones?] tried to outdo each other in the size and spectacle of their greeting. Children formed an important part of most receptions. This was in order to reinforce in a new generation the traditional ties with Britain. It was also to show off the healthy vibrancy of the country.

All was not entirely well on the tour. The Queen had been in the country for only a short time [how long?] when a rail disaster occurred [where? when?], in which a large number of people died. More problems arose when the government announced that there would be only one Maori reception for the Queen. The Minister of Maori Affairs [name?] showed insensitivity to the Maori desire to demonstrate their loyalty along tribal lines: 'So far as the Queen herself is concerned, they will just be the Maori people. She will not be concerned to know from what tribes they have come.' Initially there were no plans to attend a welcome at the base of the Maori King Movement [name?]. In the end, the government gave in and scheduled a three-minute visit. The Queen, impressed by the preparations and reception, ended up staying longer [how much longer?].

Activity 1, pp. 96–97

All are **protest** actions ('protest' is in all of these statements): **a**, **b**, **e**, **g**, **i**

Other **non-protest** actions: **c**, **d**, **f**, **h**

Activity 2, pp. 97–98

All are **protest** actions ('protest' is in all of these statements): **a**, **b**, **h**, **i**, **k**

Other **non-protest** actions: **d**, **d**, **e**, **g**

Actions around issues of law: **f**, **j**, **l**, **m**

Activity 3, pp. 99–100

Social and political control: d, **e**, **g**, **i**, **n**, **s**

Relations with Britain: a, **k**, **o**, **r**

World War Two: c, **h**, **j**, **l**, **p**, **t**, **v**

Queen Salote, 1918-1965: b, **f**, **m**, **q**, **u**, **w**

Activity 2, p.102

What Bob enjoys 1: Apples, bananas, grapes, pineapples

Topic sentence, paragraph 1: One of the things Bob enjoys is eating fruit.

What Bob enjoys 2: *Southpark, Shortland Street*, mutes TV ads, watches 2 hours per night, more on weekends

Topic sentence, paragraph 2: Another thing that Bob enjoys is watching TV.

What Bob enjoys 3: Rugby league, kilikiti, snorkelling, kayaking

Topic sentence, paragraph 3: A third thing that Bob enjoys is playing sport.

Activity 3, p. 103

1 = **e** **2** = **b** **3** = **b** **4** = **a**

Activity 4, p.104

NOTE: your responses may differ from those below, but should still be similar. Check with your teacher if you are not sure.

Possible topic sentences

- Maori and Europeans were both keen to get trade goods and resources off each other.
- Missionaries in the Bay of Islands wanted to convert Maori to Christianity and change their cultural practices.
- Growing Maori concerns made them willing to accept the idea of British officials stepping in to control European troublemakers.

Activity 1, pp. 105–106

1. **G.** Pasifika peoples were encouraged to come to New Zealand in the 1960s but in the following decade the mood changed to a more negative one.
   - 1960s
   - Pacific Island people
   - New Zealand
   - 1970s
   - 1975
   - National government
   - Polynesian Panthers
2. **C.** Young Pasifika people growing up in New Zealand in the 1970s found themselves having to live in two very different worlds.
   - Tonga, Samoa, and the Cook Islands
   - European
   - 'coconut'
3. **E.** Young Pasifika people in the 1970s responded differently to the racism they experienced.
   - Mongrel Mob
   - Hells Angels
   - schools
4. **A.** The Polynesian Panther Party (PPP) was formed by the Tongan Will 'Ilolahia to help out those who were struggling.
   - Ilolahia
   - 'Nigs'
   - Tongan, Samoan, and Cook Island
   - Maori
5. **F.** There were three key areas of concern that the Polynesian Panther Party wanted to address, and the first of these was racism.
   - Melani Anae
   - police
   - landlords
   - *'that we weren't just robbers and rapists, as the media was putting out there; that we were just migrants and their New Zealand-born children, dealing with issues of settlement (for our parents) and identity (for the youth).'*
6. **B.** The second area of concern that the Panthers wanted to address was education.
   - community homework centre
   - Ponsonby
   - 'Black Pride'
7. **D.** The third key goal of the Panthers was to unite with like-minded groups, both brown and white.
   - Nga Tamatoa
   - Maori university students
   - Peoples' Union
   - Black Power and Mongrel Mob

Activity 2, pp. 107–108

A	**3**, **g**	**B**	**6**, **c**
C	**4**, **e**	**D**	**1**, **f**
E	**2**, **b**	**F**	**7**, **a**
G	**5**, **d**		

Discuss the number of 'hard' facts in the third column with your classmates.

Activity 3, pp. 109–112

Topic A

1	**C**	**2**	**C**
3	**C**	**4**	**A**

Topic B

5	**E**	**6**	**C**
7	**A** (**B** would also be acceptable)	**8**	**B**

Activity 4, p. 114

NOTE: your responses may vary but should still be similar. Check with your teacher if you're not sure.

1 Up to the mid-1960s, many southern states in America used *laws, terror and tests* to prevent blacks from voting.

2 During the 1950s and 1960s the black civil rights movement in America carried out *non-violent protest marches and boycotts* to try to bring about change.

3 During the 1960s the Black Panther Party provided *clinics, classes and other services* to help poor blacks in urban centres.

4 During the 1960s the police in the South often responded *violently* to black civil rights protests. *(You could list some of the ways, but the word 'violently' captures the main point about police responses, according to the information provided — save the detail for the main body of the paragraph.)*

5 During the black civil rights movement of the 1960s women were typically *involved with protests, training and organising.*

6 Official laws and rulings that *ended segregation and improved rights* were the result of successful civil rights' actions after WWII. *(Again, you could provide more detail but with this outline here the detail can come in the main body of the paragraph.)*

Activities, paragraphs 1–4 (WWII), pp. 118–120

NOTE: you may have different responses to the ones given below. If so, check these with your teacher.

Paragraph 1

Another aggressive action taken by Germany which threatened peace in Europe and Asia was the attempt to unify with Austria (*Anschluss*). Germany attempted Anschluss with Austria [explain this a bit more: why?]. Hitler overestimated his power and sent troops to Austria [when?]. Italy was not happy about this and sent troops to the border of Italy and Austria. [Why?] Germany then backed down. Hitler then in response to this rearmed [give some details/facts] and announced the existence of the Luftwaffe [give some details/facts]. Other countries then responded to this by preparing themselves for defense not attack. France later built the Maginot Line in the hope that it would prevent the Germans from invading.

Point A: The topic sentence does use key words from the essay question/topic, although *perhaps* including the date of *Anschluss* would show that this event is within the timeframe of the question. ☺

Point B: The topic sentence does signal well the main point that is covered in the paragraph body: *Anschluss (the explanation of why this was an aggressive action comes in the main body of the paragraph).* The topic sentence doesn't go into unnecessary detail, leaving that for the main body of the paragraph ☺

Point C: The main body starts well but then drifts off to talking about Hitler's rearmament and announcement about the Luftwaffe (German airforce); if this is relevant to *Anschluss* in some way then it should be made clearer how. A better solution would be to include 'rearmament' in the Topic Sentence. The response of other countries/France is definitely not related to the key idea signalled in the Topic Sentence. ☹

Point D: There is not a lot of detail/information, especially considering that the last part of the paragraph is not really relevant to the topic sentence. ☹

Point E: There are a few 'hard' facts but not many… ☹

Overall comment: This is a 'bare minimum' paragraph with some material that does not relate to the main point signalled in the topic sentence.

Paragraph 2

Japan invaded the Chinese province of Manchuria in 1931 in response to an 'alleged' attack on a Japanese railway station [this would probably go better in the main body rather than here]. Japan was quickly becoming overpopulated [statistics?] and saw Manchuria as a valuable source of raw materials [such as?], as well as an ideal place for population resettlement. The Japanese government was not told of the military action. China appealed to the League of Nations [date, perhaps?] asking them to condemn Japan as an aggressor. The League of Nations sent the Lytton Commission to investigate, headed by Lord Lytton (Britain). Japan was declared the aggressor by the Commission, although no trade or economic sanctions were applied. Angered, Japan withdrew from the League in 1933. Unstopped, Japan continued to expand into China and by 1937 had occupied coastal and other large areas of China moving towards the south.

Point A: There isn't much in the way of reference to the essay topic/question; the topic sentence must use key words from the essay topic/question to show that it is answering it. ☹

Point B: We do know the key point to be covered in the main body of the paragraph: Japan's invasion of Manchuria, which is within the timeframe of the essay topic/question. ☺

Point C: All of the information is in fact relevant to what is signalled in the topic sentence, although it would have been better if the topic sentence mentioned how the weak response of the League of Nations further encouraged Japan, as otherwise this information is not specifically about Japan's aggressive actions. 😐

Point D: There is reasonably good depth and detail here.

Point E: Apart from the points noted, the 'hard' facts here are quite good: names of people, places and organisations, plus some dates. ☺

Overall comment: Apart from the poor topic sentence this paragraph is quite strong; the addition of a few more 'hard' facts would make it even stronger.

Paragraph 3

Another action which led to tension in Europe was Germany's rearmament. A disarmament conference [organised by?] was held in 1932 for countries to discuss ways in which they could disarm. France was uneasy about Germany's presence and the tensions between the two led to Hitler leaving the conference and withdrawing from the League. Hitler then began to rearm at great speed. According to the Treaty of Versailles, Germany was only allowed an army of 100,000 men, no conscription and no airforce (among other conditions). In 1935 Hitler announced that he had created a new German Luftwaffe (airforce) and had introduced conscription to bring his army to 500,000 men. Both these actions were against the Treaty of Versailles and threatened peace in Europe.

Point A: The topic sentence does use key words from the essay question/topic, although *perhaps* including the date that rearmament began or was announced would show that this event is within the timeframe of the question. ☺

Point B: The topic sentence does signal well the main point that is covered in the paragraph body: *<u>German rearmament</u> (the explanation of why this was an aggressive action comes in the main body of the paragraph).* The Topic Sentence doesn't go into unnecessary detail, leaving that for the main body of the paragraph ☺

Point C: All of the paragraph's explanation and examples are related to the one main idea as signalled in the topic sentence (Germany's rearmament). ☺

Point D: There is good depth and detail here (although perhaps they could have mentioned who organised the disarmament conference — the League of Nations). The paragraph wraps up nicely by referring back to the essay topic/question, making it clear how German rearmament increased tension by threatening the peace. ☺

Point E: The 'hard' facts here are quite good: names of people, places and organisations, plus some dates and statistics. ☺

Overall comment: This is a well-written, detailed paragraph with good supporting evidence that is focused around the key point signalled in the topic sentence and thus helps answer the essay topic/question. ☺

Paragraph 4

While all eyes were focused on Abyssinia, Hitler took yet another aggressive move [that further increased tension in Europe]. He occupied the Rhineland [when? And explain briefly what is significant about the Rhineland]. This was a direct breach of the Locarno Pact of 1925 and the Treaty of Versailles, which stated that the Rhineland must remain demilitarised *[no weapons allowed]*. Hitler's reason for doing this was simple. He wanted to see if Britain and France would stop him. [why

 ISBN: 9780170352581

would/should they?] He wanted to know how far he could push them. His gamble paid off. The French offered no resistance [why not?] and Germany overran the Rhineland. The unification of all German people had begun. Next, Japan slowly took over the province of Manchuria in China, which they renamed Manchukuo. Finally in 1937, Japan began a full invasion of China. This, again, threatened peace in Europe and increased the already building tensions.

Point A: This topic sentence is actually quite good at linking from the previous paragraph's main point onto the main point in this one (assuming that the preceding paragraph had been about the crisis in Abyssinia, created by Italy's actions). Adding in the highlighted words connects this topic sentence more clearly to the essay topic/question. However, see also Point B below.

Point B: 'He occupied the Rhineland' is an 'orphan sentence' that should have been part of the topic sentence; if it had been then the topic sentence would have been signalling clearly what the 'aggressive move' was that Hitler next made. ☹

Point C: The main body starts very well and is clearly focused on the main point signalled in the topic sentence (the modified version: *occupation of the Rhineland*). However, the highlighted sentences should not have been in this paragraph as they are on a completely different set of events. The final sentence is good at linking back to the topic sentence and essay topic/ question. 😐

Point D: The depth and detail here for the occupation of the Rhineland is good, although a little further explanation as noted would have helped. 😐

Point E: There are *some* good 'hard' facts here but a few more would have improved this further. ☺

Overall comment: This is not a bad paragraph although there are still a few things to fix up. 😐

Activities, paragraphs 1–3 (Ireland), pp.121–123

Paragraph 1

In the 1916 Easter Rising, only a handful of Irish 'rebel' leaders were actually informed of the rebellion, and the main backer of the rebellion was Patrick Pearse, leader of the revolutionary 'Fenians', otherwise known as the Irish Republican Brotherhood (IRB). It was Pearse's hope that the rebellion [where?] would bring a fully independent Ireland, free from British control. [Perhaps provide a little explanation of why this was a desired goal.] His idea was that in order for their country to be free, people (in this case the rebels) would have to sacrifice their lives for Ireland, with hope that an emotionally driven Irish public would remember their cause and fight radically for an Irish republic. This idea was known as, in Pearse's own words, a 'blood sacrifice'. Pearse also planned such a rebellion to take place during Easter, an important time for Catholics in which they remember the resurrection of Jesus. Through the significance of the occasion, he hoped it would also symbolise the resurrection or rebirth of an independent Irish republic.

Point A: This is a terrible topic sentence! It has very little connection to the essay topic/question and is far too long. Start again! ☹

Point B: It is not at all clear what exactly will be the focus of the main body of this paragraph, in terms of what the leaders hoped to achieve. ☹

Point C: *If* the topic sentence had signalled more clearly that this paragraph was to be about what Patrick Pearse, leader of the Fenians/IRB, hoped to achieve then the main body has focused on this quite well. ☺

Point D: The depth and detail on what Pearse hoped to achieve is good and does help us clearly understand his reasons/goals. ☺

Point E: There is a variety of good 'hard' facts (although some of those in the topic sentence would have been better in the main body), including a nice short quote from Pearse ('blood sacrifice'). Perhaps adding in where the rebellion was set to take place and how many Fenians/IRB members there were would have improved this. ☺

Overall comment: Apart from the terrible topic sentence the rest of this paragraph is good and develops the goals of Pearse with reasonable detail/ explanation. 😐

Paragraph 2

Patrick Pearse, who was the leader of the 1916 Easter uprising [where?], hoped that the planned date of Easter Sunday would create a patriotic feeling amongst the Irish and they would rise up against the British. However, the ship the *Aud* that was carrying 20,000 obsolete *[out-dated]* German rifles for the uprising was captured and sunk by the British. Also, the soldiers that Pearse was relying on using, the Irish Volunteers [how many?], had been told by their own leader not to support the Rising [briefly, why not?]. Patrick Pearse and the other rebel military leaders realised that the Uprising would not have much success and the planned date of Easter Sunday was postponed until Easter Monday. Pearse decided to use yet another of the small [how small?] Irish military groups that were opposed to British rule. James Connelly's Citizens' Army and Pearse's Irish Republican Brotherhood finally set out on their own to fight the British on Easter Monday. Because both armies were small [how many?] and hopelessly outnumbered by the British [how many?], the Military Council came up with the idea of a 'blood sacrifice'. It was hoped that many of the soldiers would die for the cause and create a wave of support around Ireland for their cause.

Point A: The topic sentence is clearly linked to what the essay topic/ question is asking. ☺

Point B: We are given a clear signal as to what is going to be the main focus of the rest of the paragraph: Patrick Pearse's hopes. Perhaps the highlighted detail could have gone into the main body of the paragraph. ☺

Point C: Although this seems impressive with its depth and detail, the information here has drifted away somewhat from answering 'what did Pearse hope to achieve' to answering instead 'what happened/what went wrong'. The last two sentences do bring the focus back to what it should be. The sort of 'slightly off-topic' material that has been included is fine *if the link to the essay topic/question is clearly stated.* 😐

Point D: This has good depth/detail, although see Point C above. 😐

Point E: The 'hard' facts are quite good: names of people, places and organisations, plus some dates and statistics, as well as the short quote from Pearse ('blood sacrifice'). A few more as noted would improve this further. ☺

Overall comment: If the writer had better linked the detail provided on *what happened* and *what went wrong* to what the essay topic/question had asked (*the aims of the Easter Rising leaders*) then this would have been a very strong and detailed paragraph. 😐

Paragraph 3

James Connolly, leader of the Irish Citizen's Army (ICA) during the 1916 Easter Rising, wanted Ireland not only to be free of British rule but also free of class divisions. Connolly had returned from the United States [to where in Ireland?] in 1910 committed to improving the poor conditions of the Irish workers, made worse, as he saw it, by 'British greed'. To carry out this fight he became General Secretary of the Irish Transport and General Workers' Union in 1914, as well as leader of the ICA. The ICA believed in violence as a necessary means to achieving an Irish republic. Like the Irish Republican Brotherhood, led by Patrick Pearse, this militia of just 220 men were active revolutionaries. Connolly, however, did not agree with Pearse's belief in a pointless 'blood sacrifice'. He believed in a full Marxist revolution: 'governments are nothing more than committees of the rich' he said. In January 1916 Connolly finally agreed to join with Pearse in the rebellion. In terms of military goals, it was hoped that the soldiers would be able to capture key places around Dublin, such as Dublin Castle (the British headquarters) and Bollands Mill, which would make it harder for the British soldiers to crush the uprising.

Point A: Excellent topic sentence! It clearly responds to the essay topic/ question. ☺

Point B: The topic sentence does signal very well the main point that is covered in the paragraph body: the goals of ICA leader James Connolly. There is no unnecessary detail that belongs in the main body.

Point C: The main body focuses very well on what is signalled in the topic sentence. Where Paragraph 2 had detail that was not linked well to the topic sentence, the background on Connolly is made relevant by being clearly linked to his goals during the Rising. Excellent! ☺

Point D: Excellent depth and detail, all of which is relevant! ☺

Point E: Excellent use of 'hard' facts: names of people, places and organisations, plus some dates and statistics, as well as a short quote from Pearse and two from Connolly. ☺

Overall comment: This is an excellent paragraph that is clearly focused throughout on the essay topic/question. There is plenty of detail/explanation and supporting evidence. ☺

Activity 1, pp. 125–126

Topic A: Conflict in Ireland

1. **Best Introduction. It covers briefly all the main points in the topic sentences.**
2. This one focuses mainly on the Irish Nationalist Party and British Prime Minister on the one hand, and the opposition of the Conservative Party and Ulster Unionists on the other.
3. This is good but focuses only on the goals of the various Irish nationalist groups.
4. This focuses only on the views/actions of the British Conservative Party and Ulster Unionists.
5. This one is reasonable but it is *too* brief and doesn't really signal enough of what is coming up in the main body of the essay.

Topic B: The end of World War One

1. This Introduction focuses firstly on the 'unfairness' of the Treaty of Versailles 'forced' on Germany, so that is what we would expect to hear about. The second part focuses only on the US.
2. **Best Introduction. It covers briefly all the main points in the topic sentences.**
3. This focuses only on France's view, and outlines (rather vaguely) that there were punishments in the Treaty of Versailles.
4. This focuses only on Britain's goals and Germany's actions with regards to its Navy. The second part is good and covers well the last two topic sentences/sets of paragraph information.
5. This Introduction outlines a focus on how Germany felt about a particular clause *[part]* of the Treaty (the 'war guilt' clause), and then onto something quite different: Hitler's desire to overturn the Treaty once in power.

Activity 2, pp.126–129

Introduction 1

Likely essay topic: Part 1

Describe the aggressive moves made by Italy, Japan and Germany during the period 1931-37 that threatened to break the peace

Likely main points (key ideas)

- Japan invaded Manchuria
- Italy invaded Abyssinia
- Germany remilitarized the Rhineland and rearmed

Likely essay topic: Part 2

Describe the actions taken by other countries and the League of Nations to deal with the aggressive nations during this period.

Likely main points (key ideas)

- protested
- no further actions

Introduction 2

Likely essay topic: Part 1

Describe the ways in which the peace settlement after World War I (WWI) caused ill feeling between Germany and the Allies.

Likely main points (key ideas)

Germany felt that it had been forced to accept a peace treaty that was:

- humiliating
- too harsh

Likely essay topic: Part 2

Describe how relationships between European countries improved between 1924 and 1929.

Likely main points (key ideas)

- Germany began to 'fulfill' the terms of the Treaty of Versailles
- a series of pacts and treaties settled post-war differences

Introduction 3

Likely essay topic: Part 1

Describe what the leaders of the 1916 Easter uprising hoped to achieve.

Likely main points (key ideas)

- a country-wide revolt against British rule
- formation of an Irish republic

Likely essay topic: Part 2

Describe the outcome of the failed Easter Rising.

Likely main points (key ideas)

- harsh response of [Britain's] General Maxwell
- growth of anti-British feeling in Southern Ireland
- formation a new political party and military group to continue the struggle

Introduction 4

Likely essay topic: Part 1

Describe the aims of the African American civil rights movement.

Likely main points (key ideas)

To obtain for African Americans the same rights that were guaranteed to all Americans in the Constitution:

- economic
- political
- social

Likely essay topic: Part 2

Describe the various groups engaged in the civil rights movement.

Likely main points (key ideas)

- moderate/non-violent: Southern Christian Leadership Conference
- radical: Black Panther Party
- radical: Black Muslims.

Summary

- The Introduction to an essay responds directly, clearly and briefly to what the essay topic/question asks. It does this by both using *key words* form the essay topic/question and also *signalling* what main points will be covered in the main body of the essay.
- 'Hard' facts are like the evidence used in a court trial; they prove a general statement/explanation that is made in the main body of a paragraph. In this way they support each paragraph's main point.
- Explain the way in which a paragraph topic sentence is similar to an essay introduction. Just as an introduction uses *key words* form the essay topic/question and also *signals* what main points will be covered in the main body of the essay, a topic sentence also uses *key words* form the essay topic/question and also *signals* what *one main point* will be covered in the main body of the paragraph.

 ISBN: 9780170352581